Much love to my two wonderful children who have been my greatest inspiration. You are the color of my life!
and
A special thank you to Mutti and Pa for all of the love you showed and gave me. I will always hold your heart in mine.

Coloring a Mindful Journey
Artistically Express Yourself Through Color

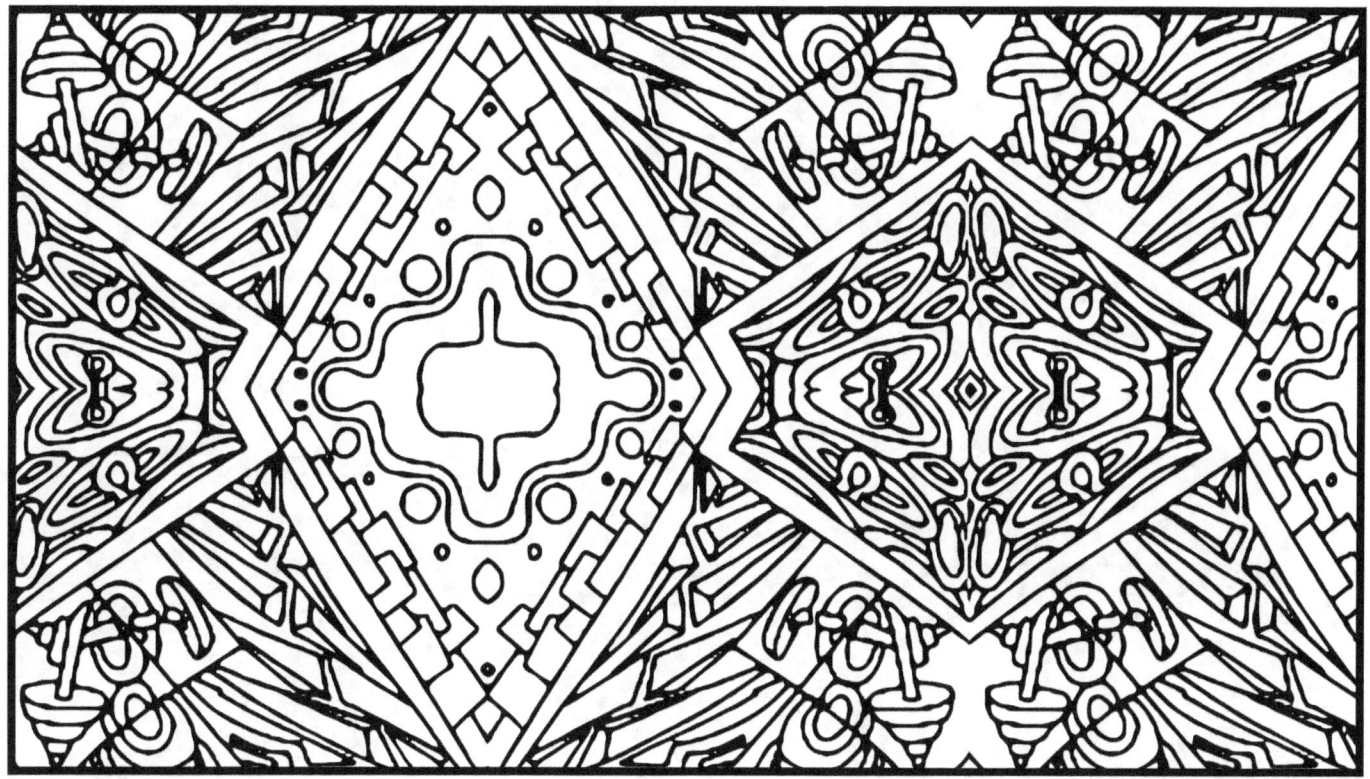

Sasha Scully is a professional artist who specializes in oil paintings, digital art, graphic design, teaching art, and using art and color as a tool for relaxation and self-discovery. With a rich background in the arts and engineering, she has shown her artwork in many different galleries and exhibits, juried art shows, been featured in several publications, and crafted award-winning art pieces.

As a mother of two and a professional artist living in New Mexico, she strives to create emotions through her work. She encourages others to do the same and create their own visual journeys through life. She uses painting, drawing, and coloring as a safe outlet for her feelings. Coloring and art is about how you feel with-in while you are creating. Embrace your feelings and enjoy living in the moment.

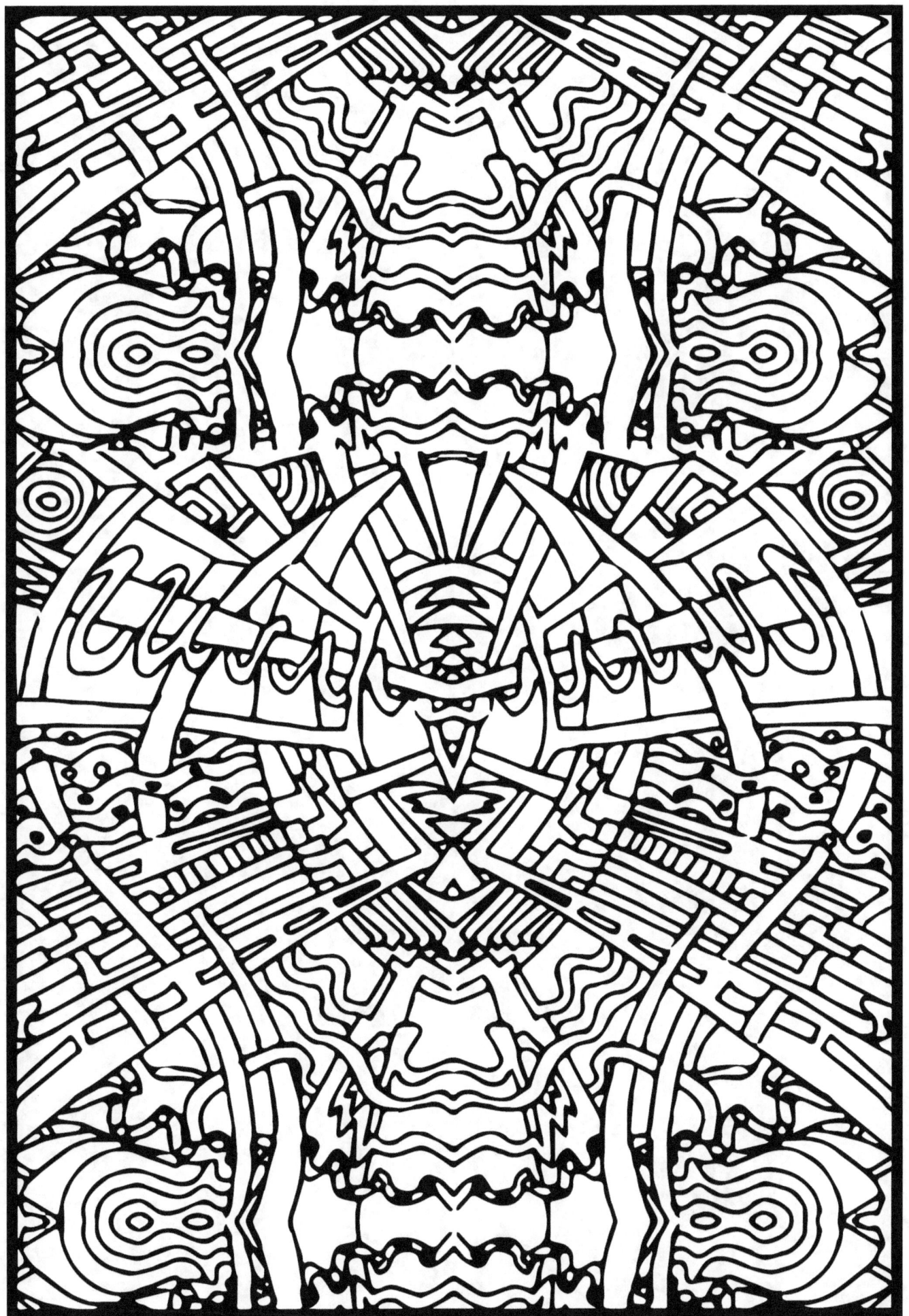

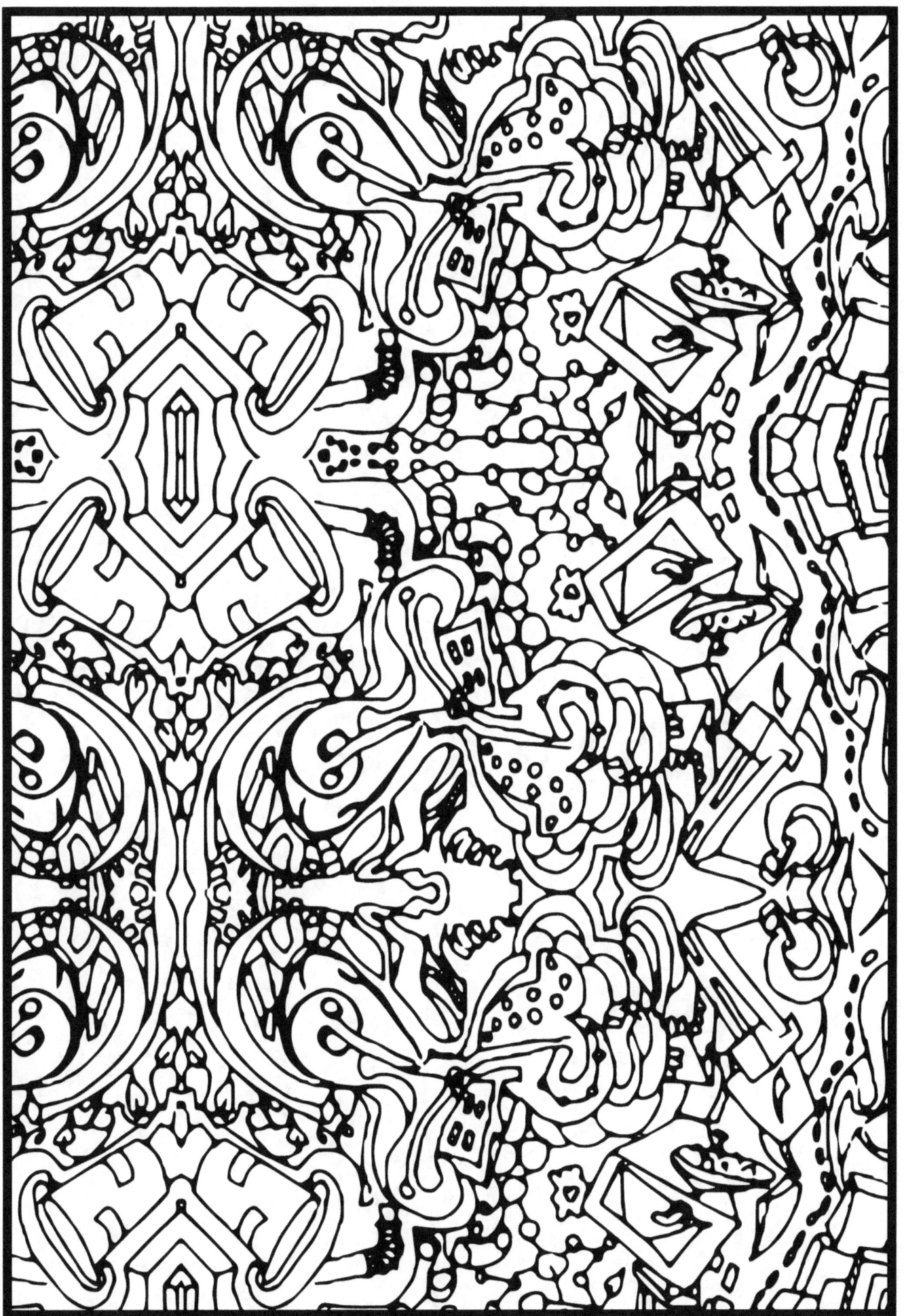

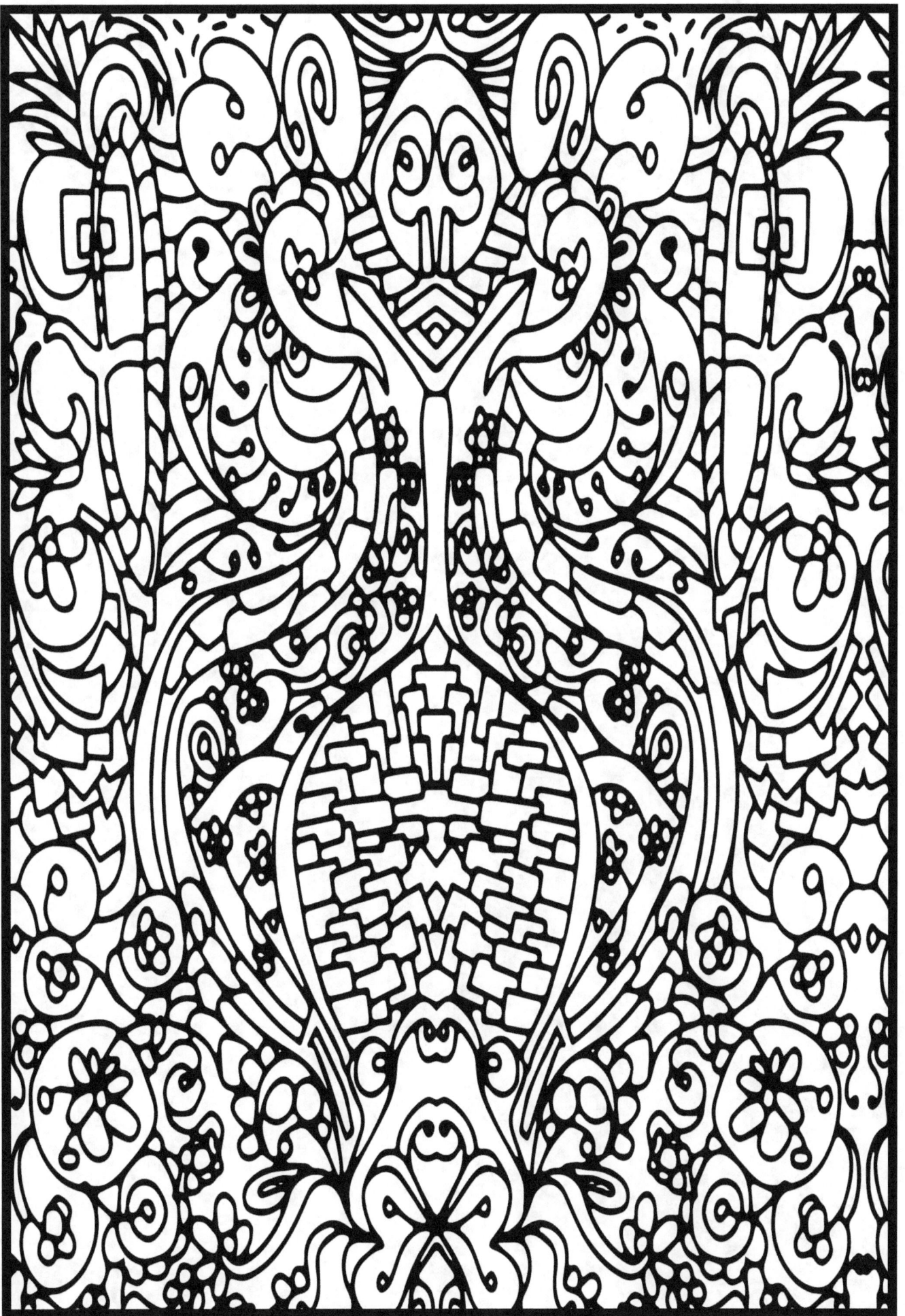

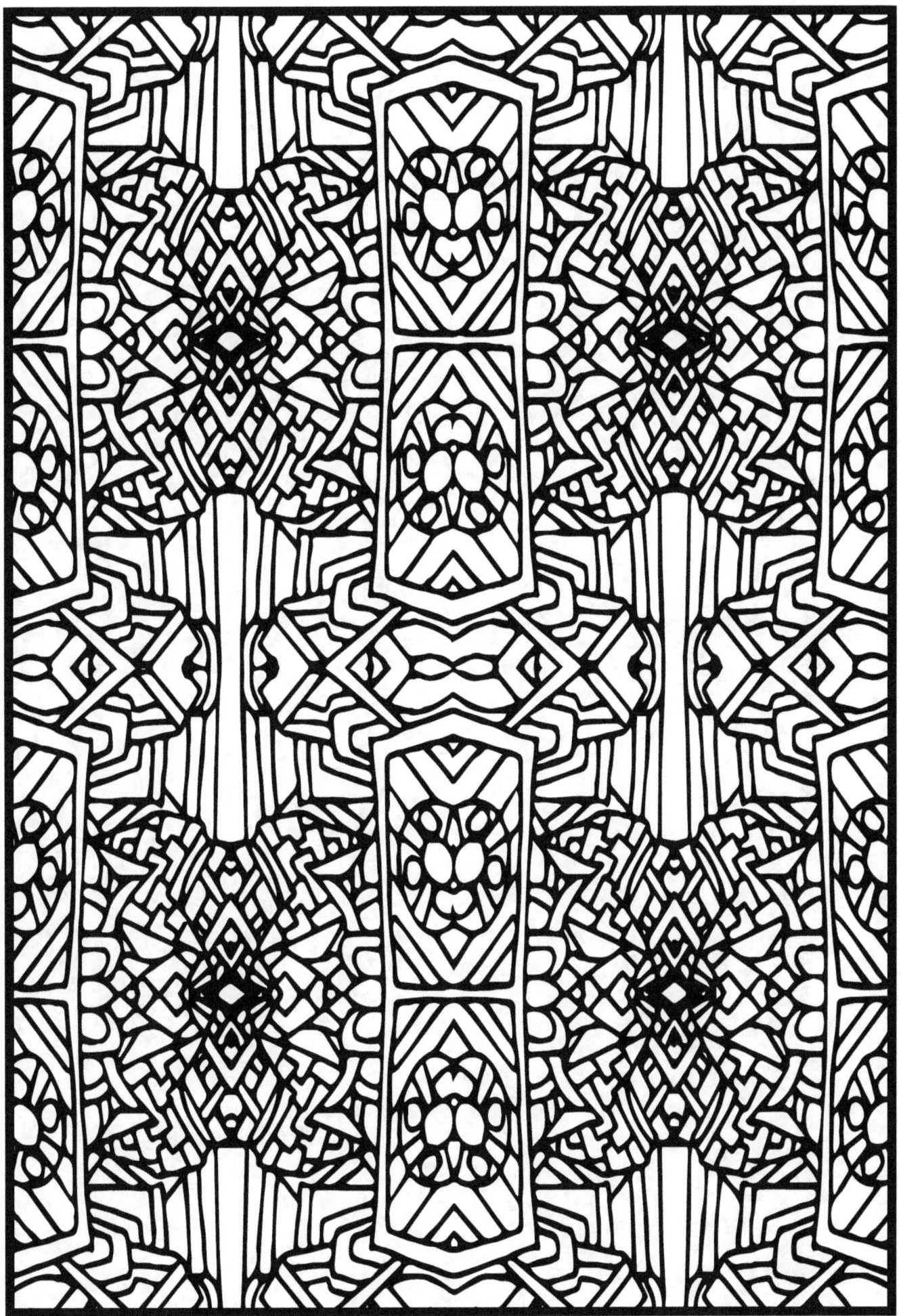

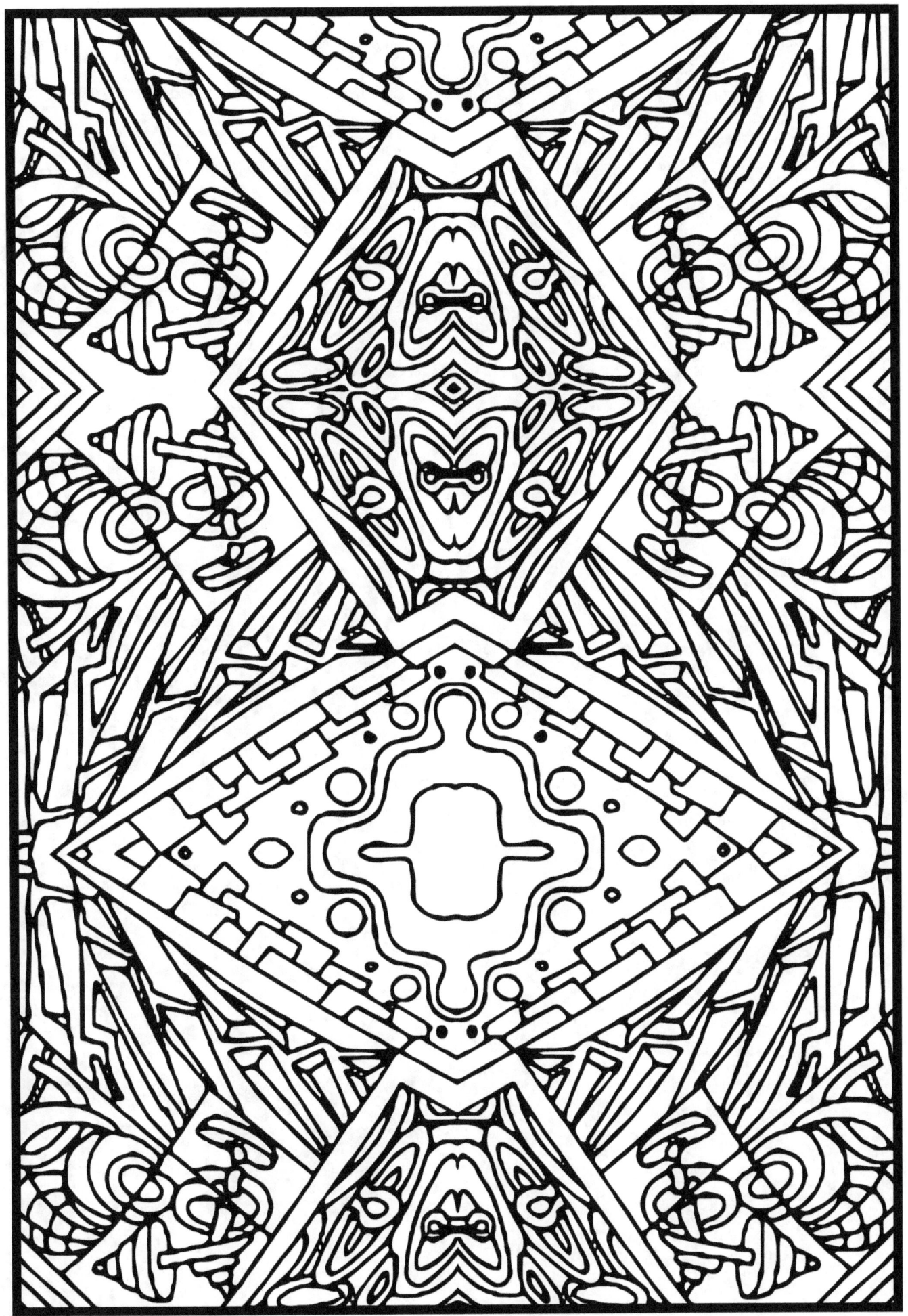

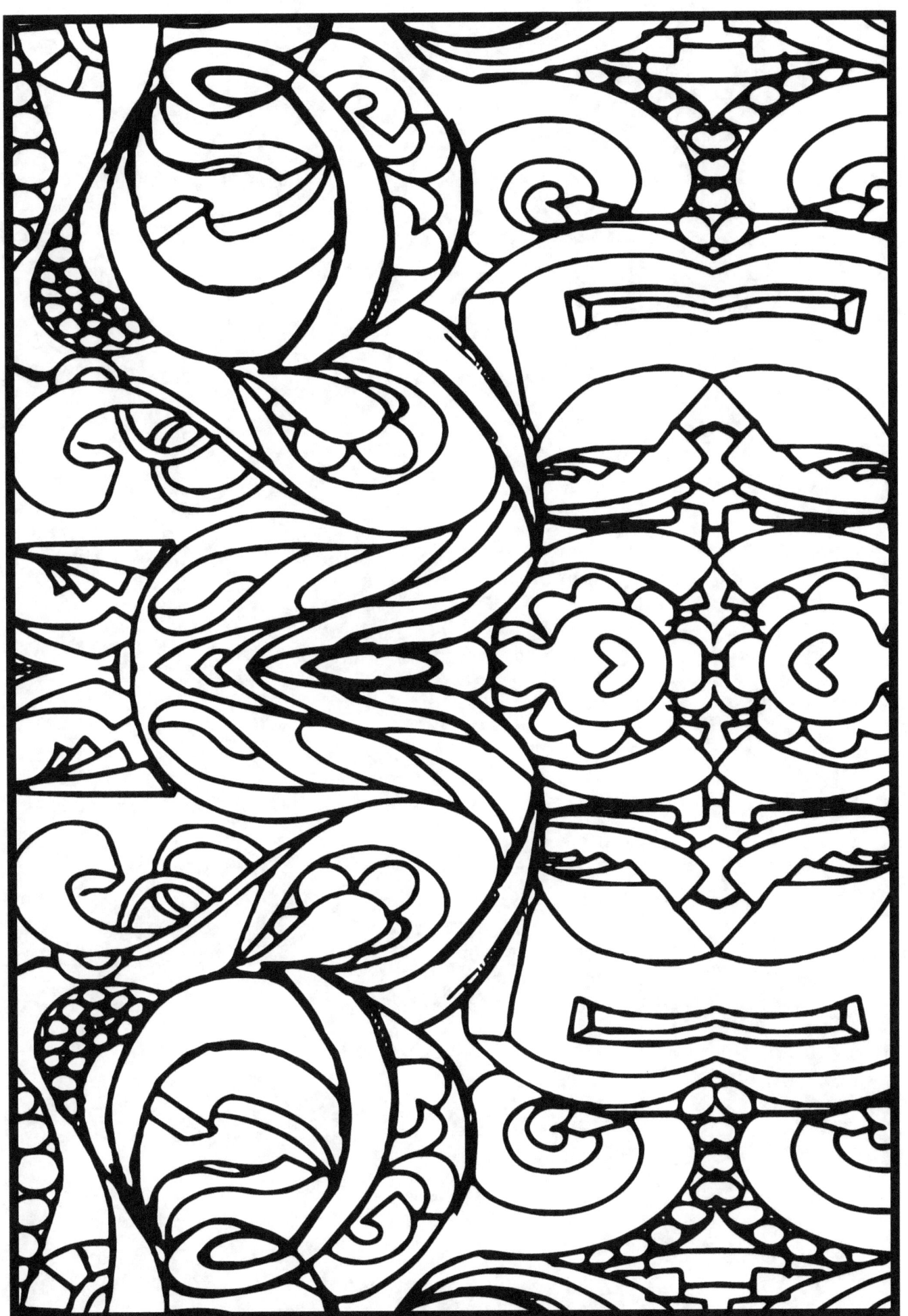

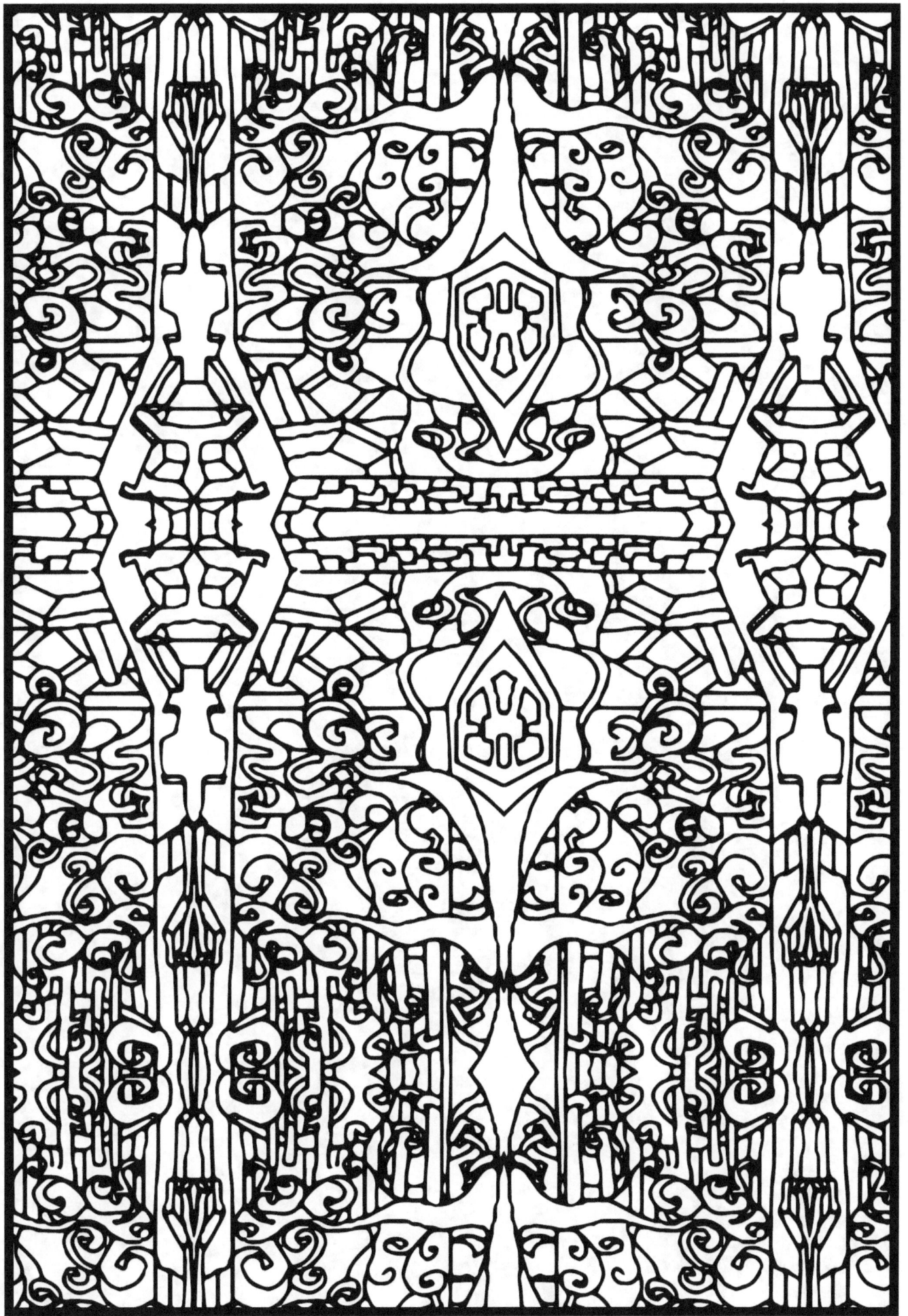

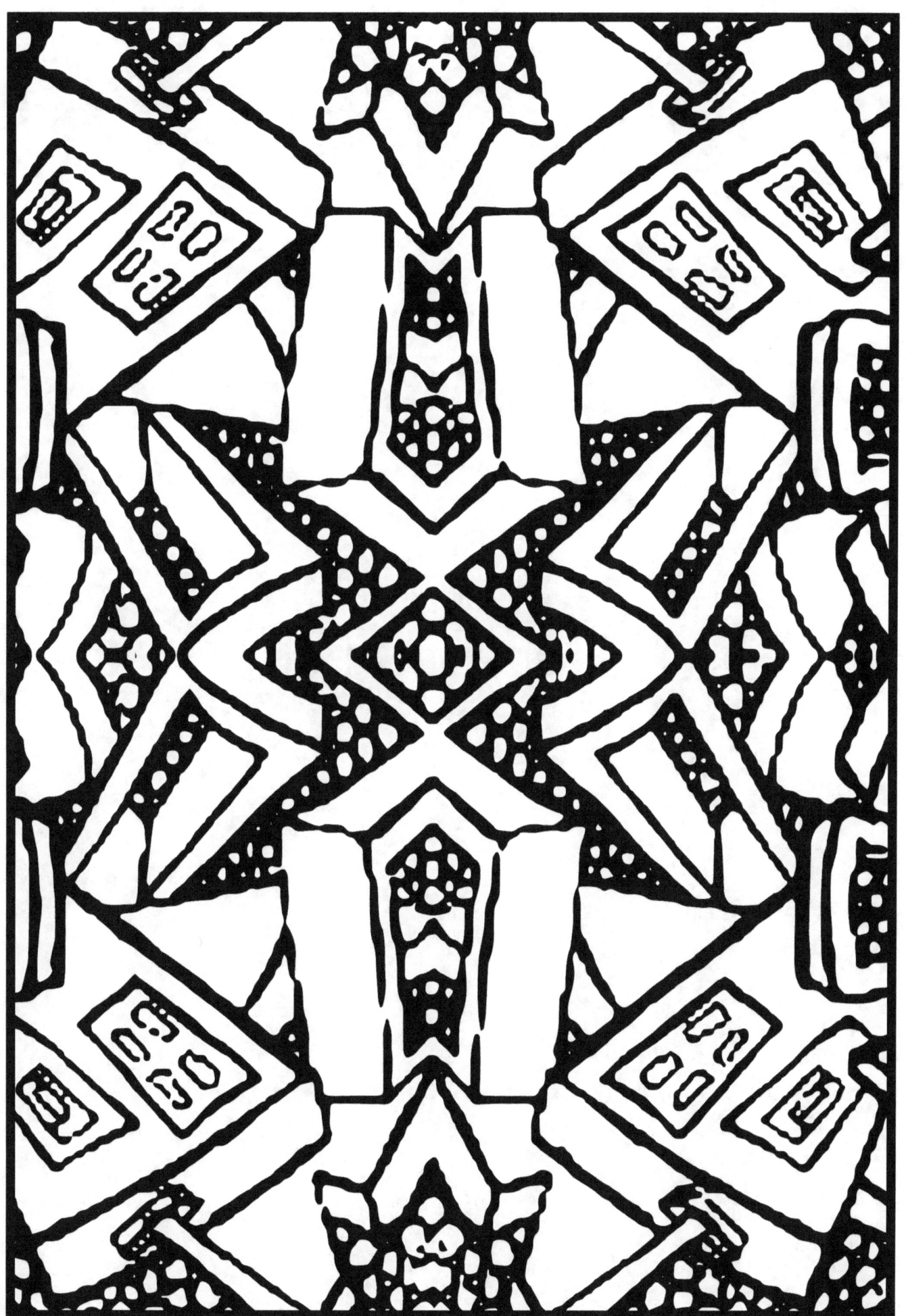

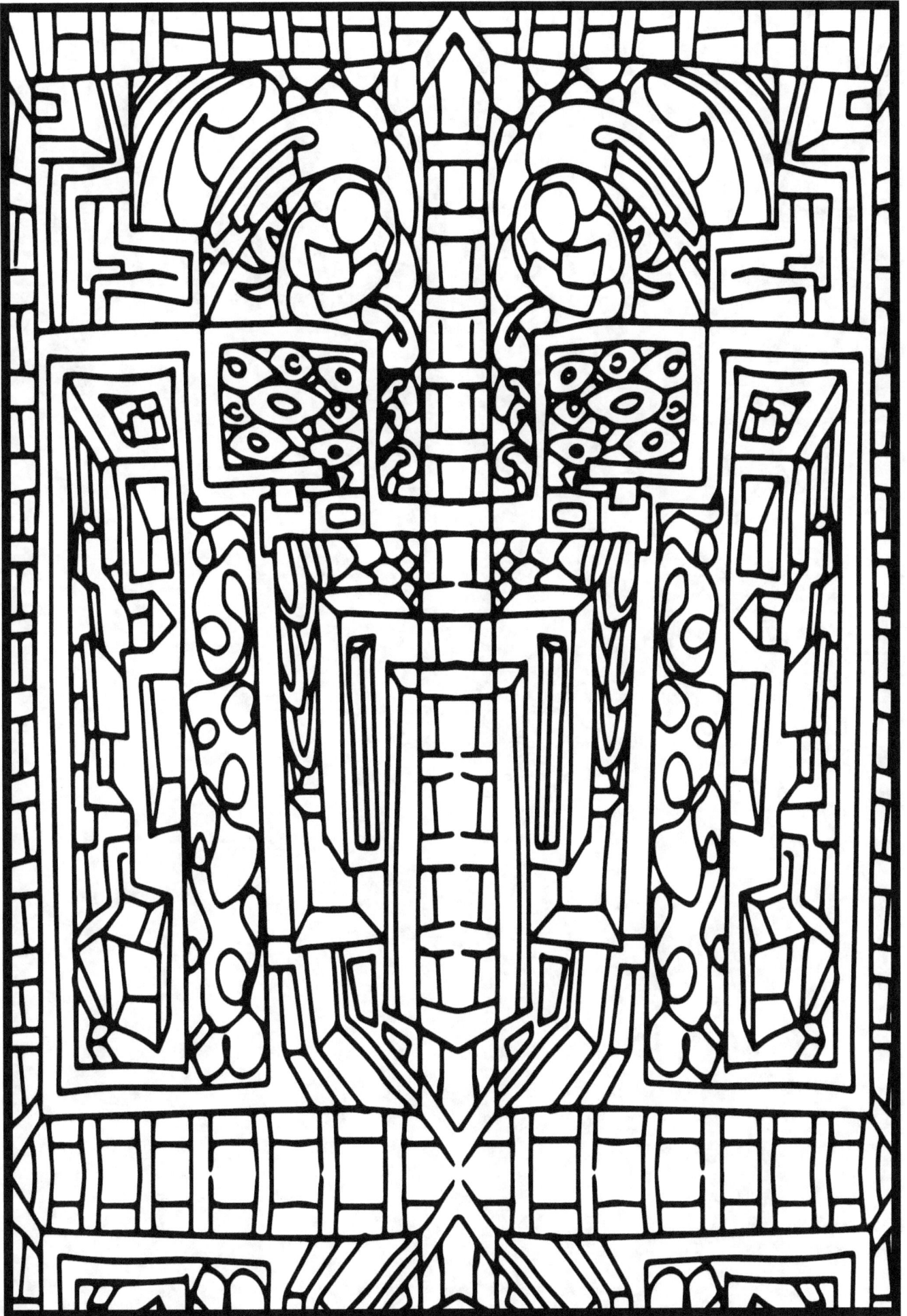

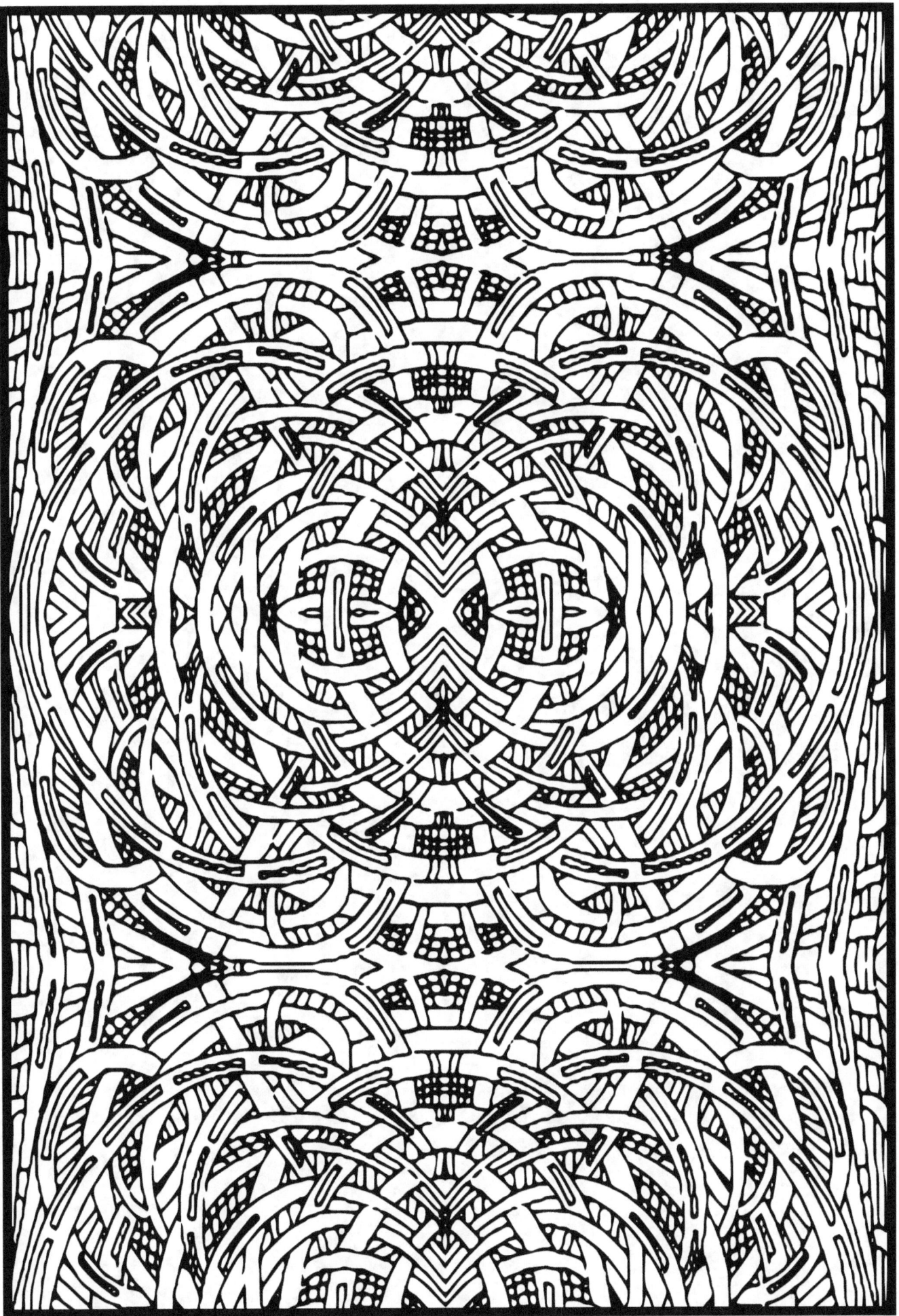

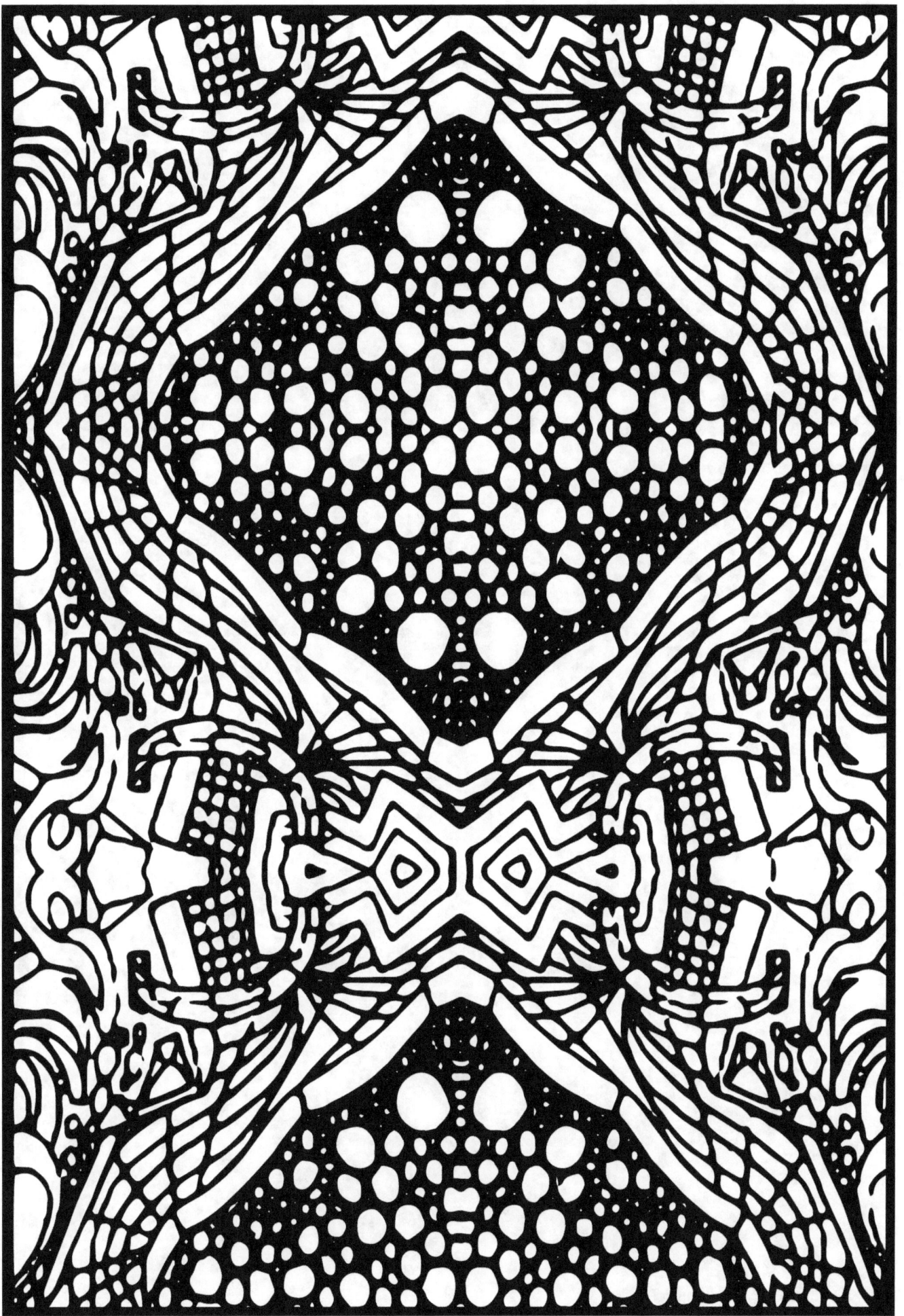

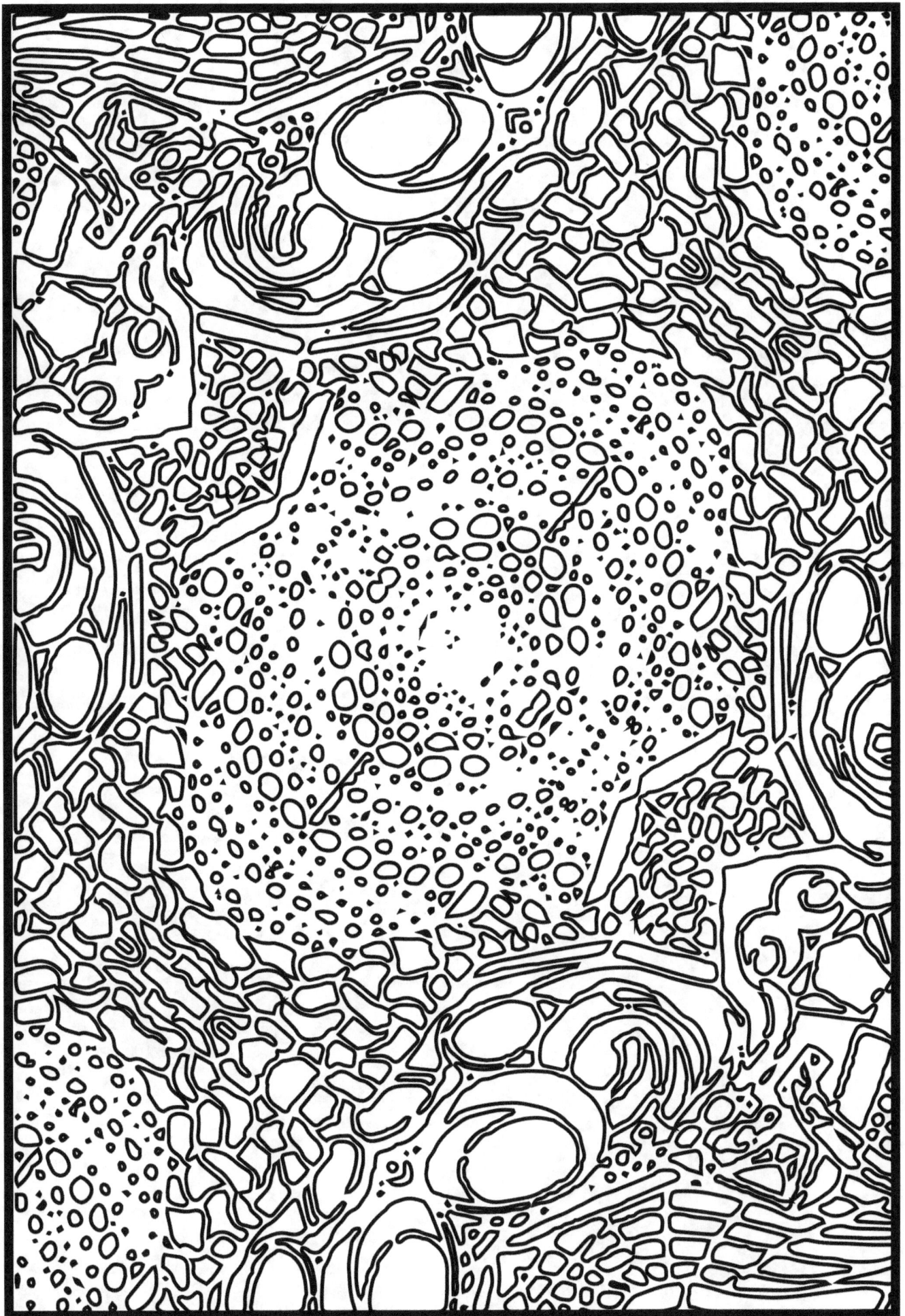

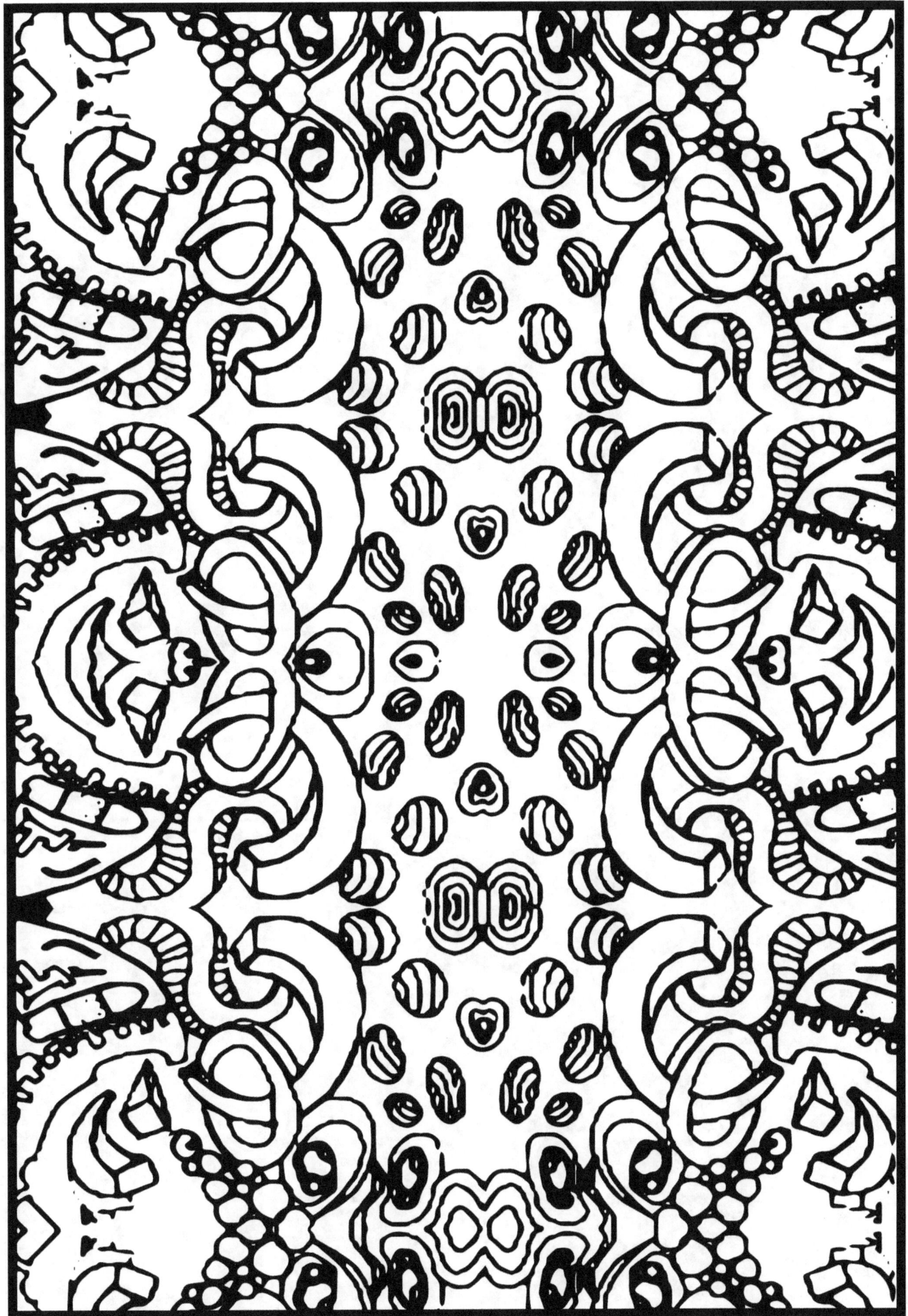

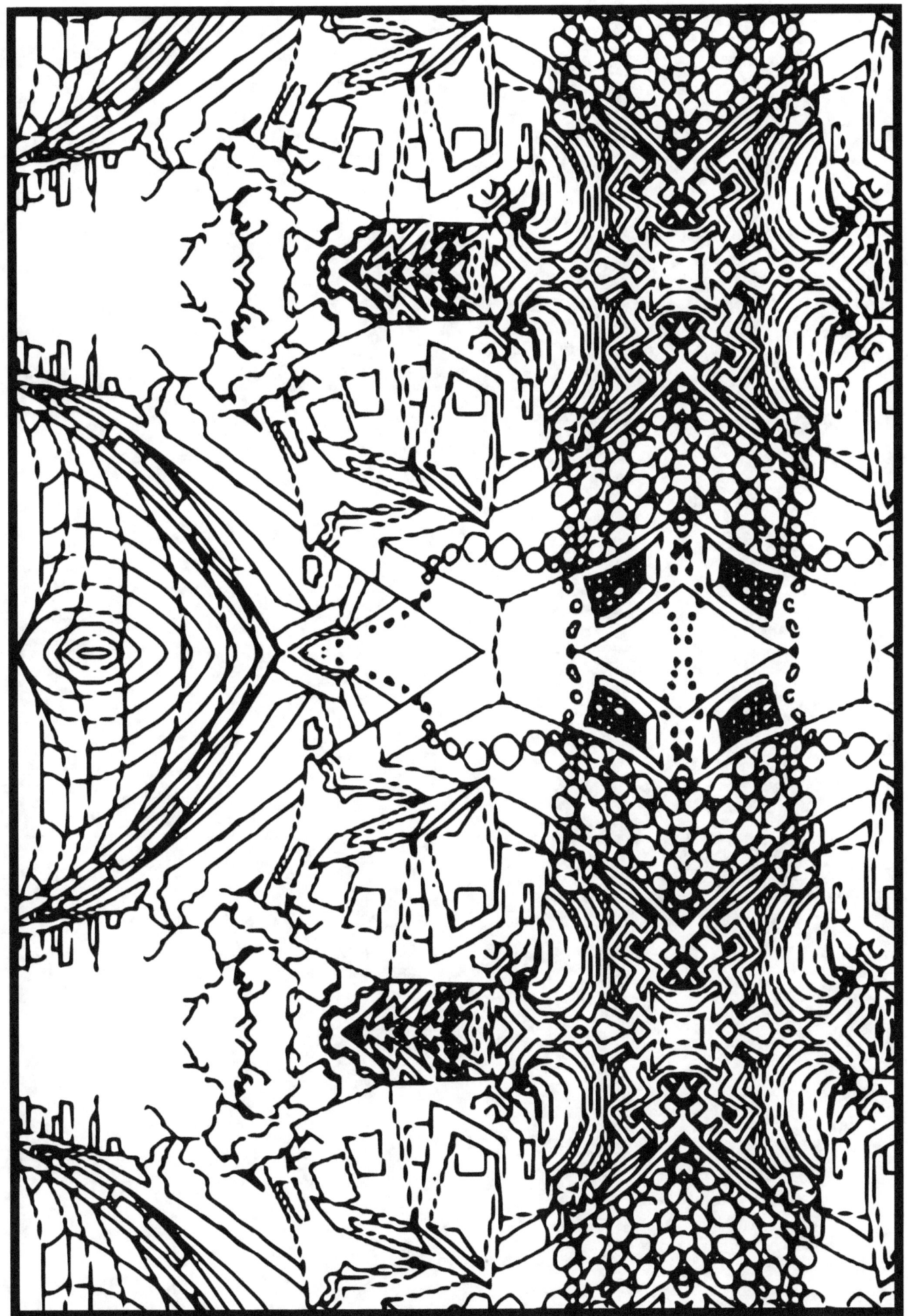

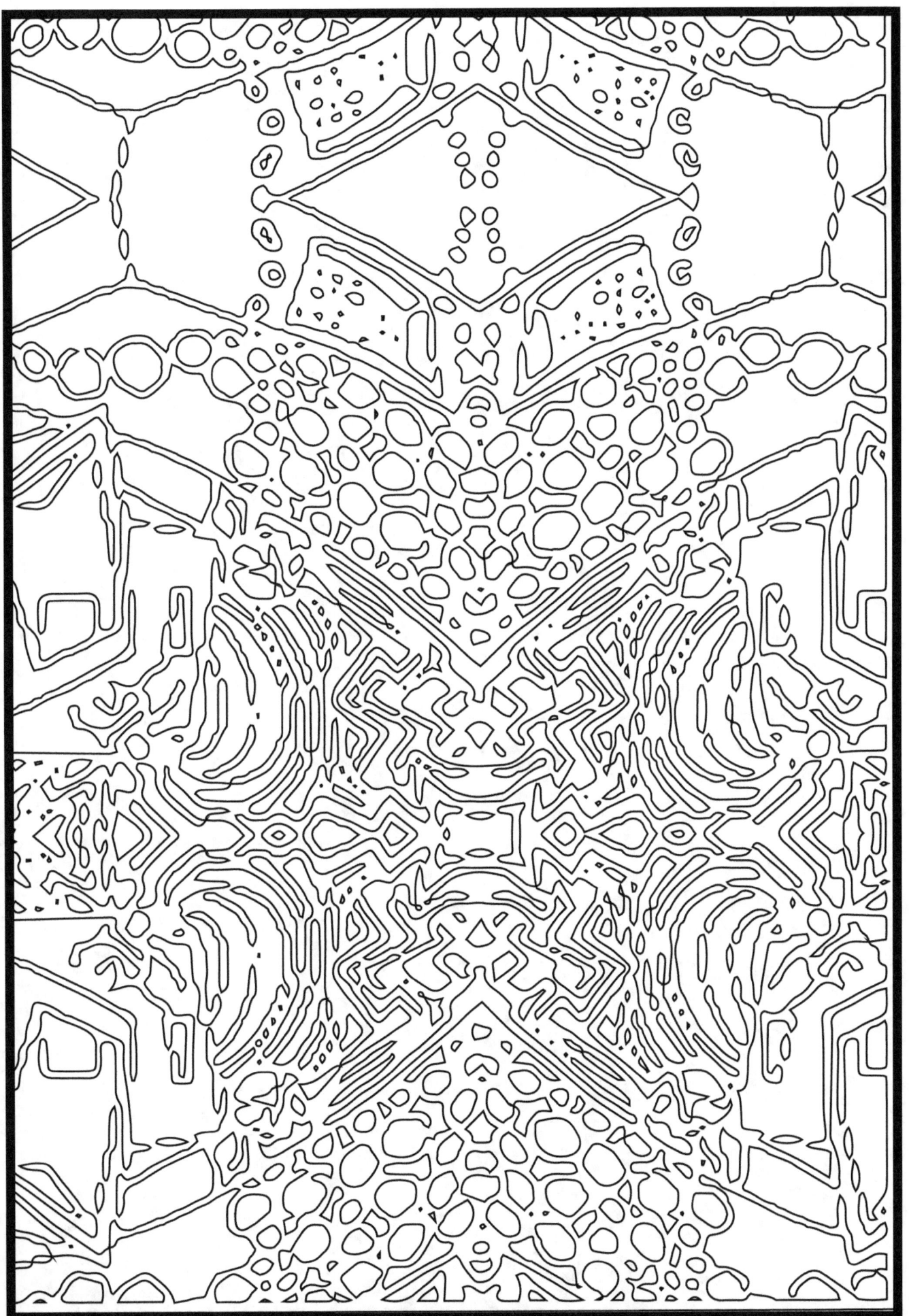

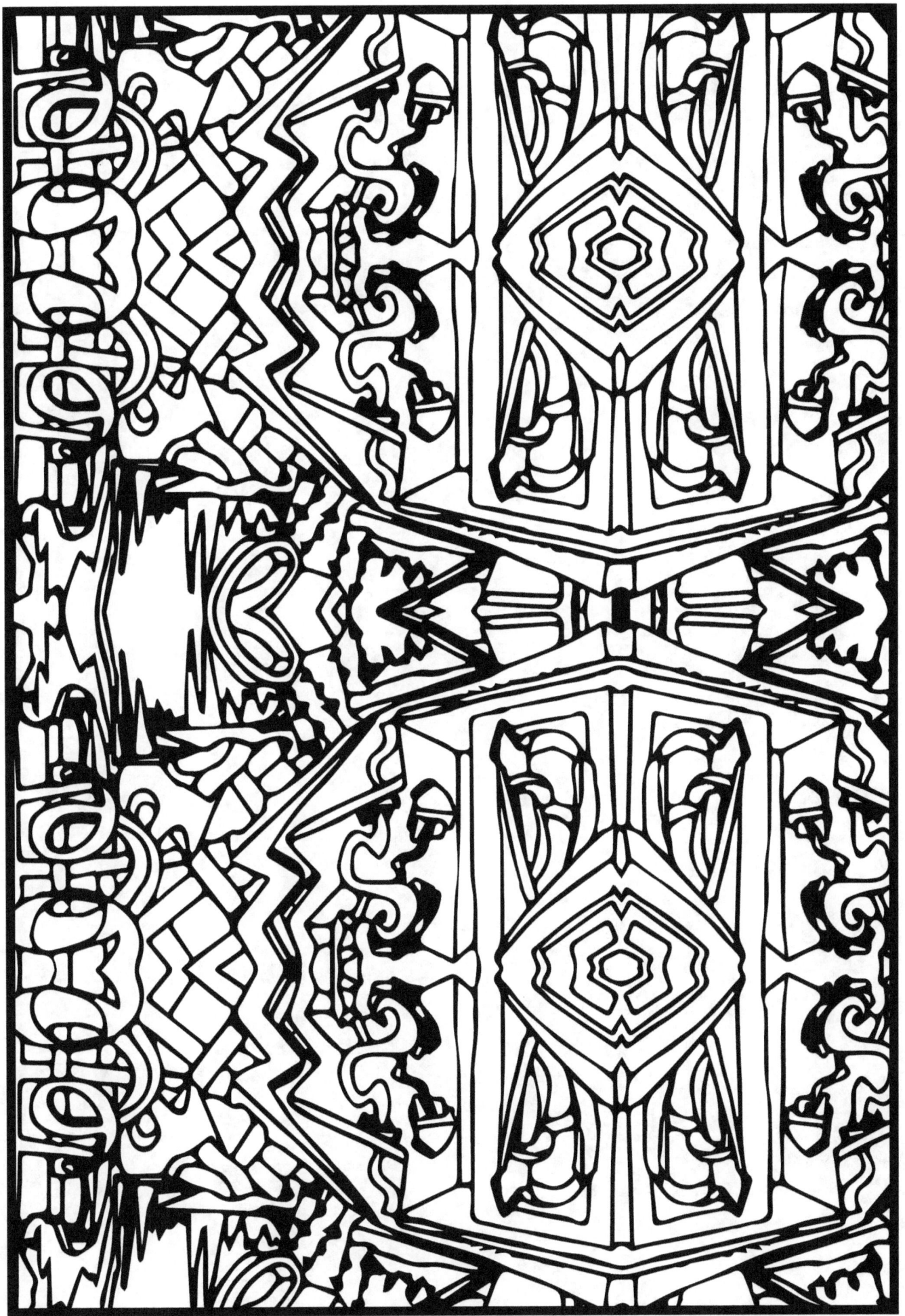

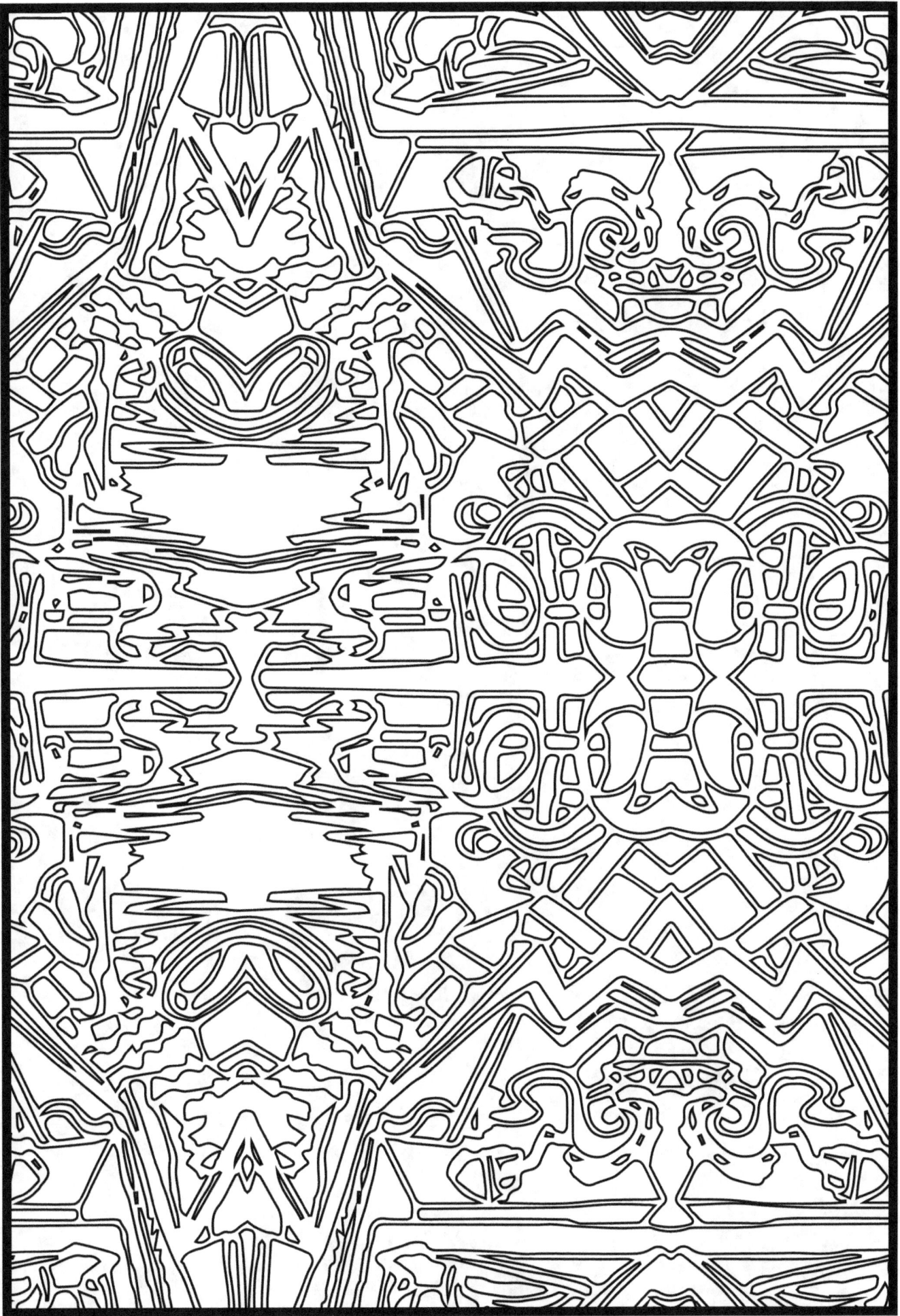

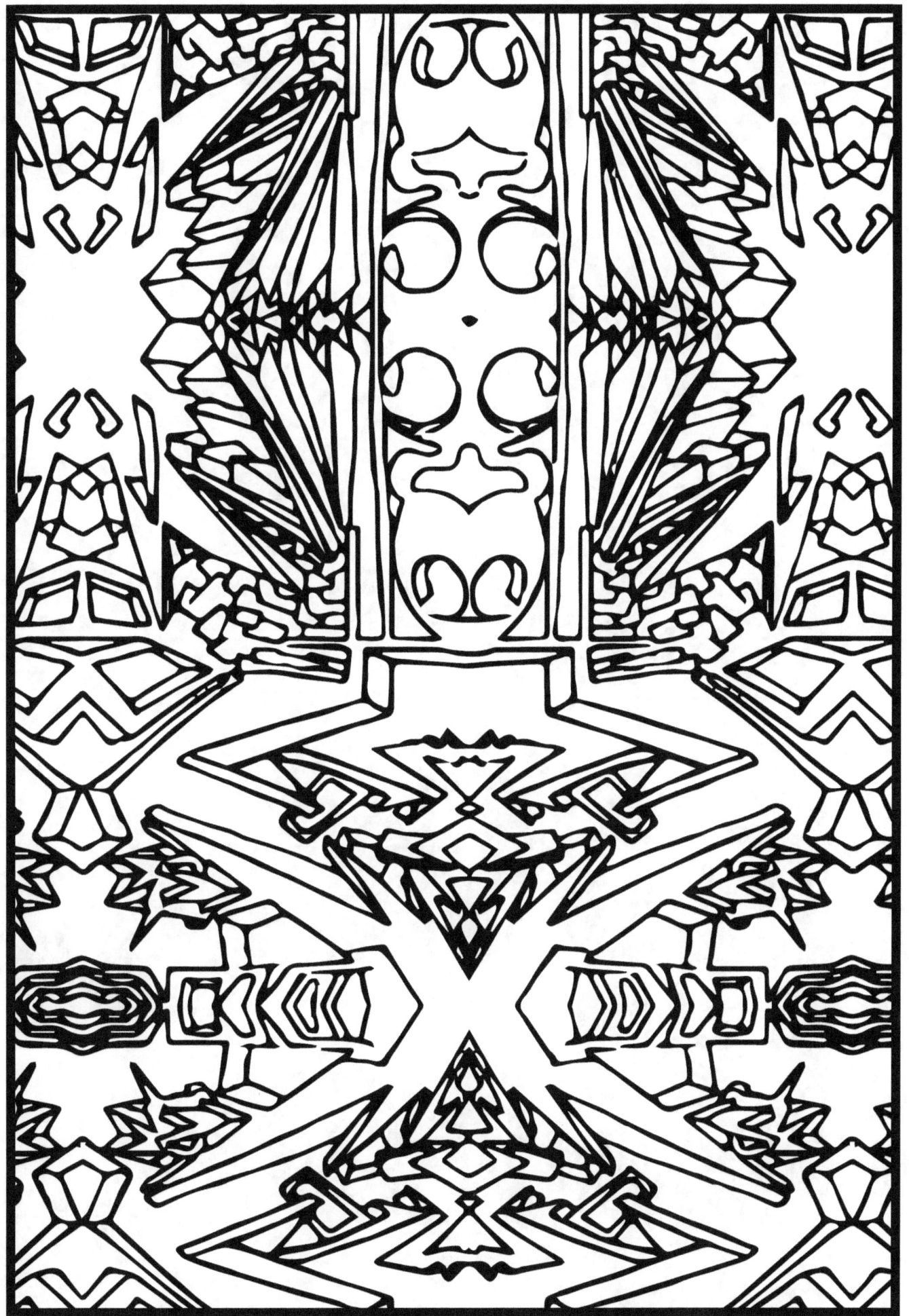

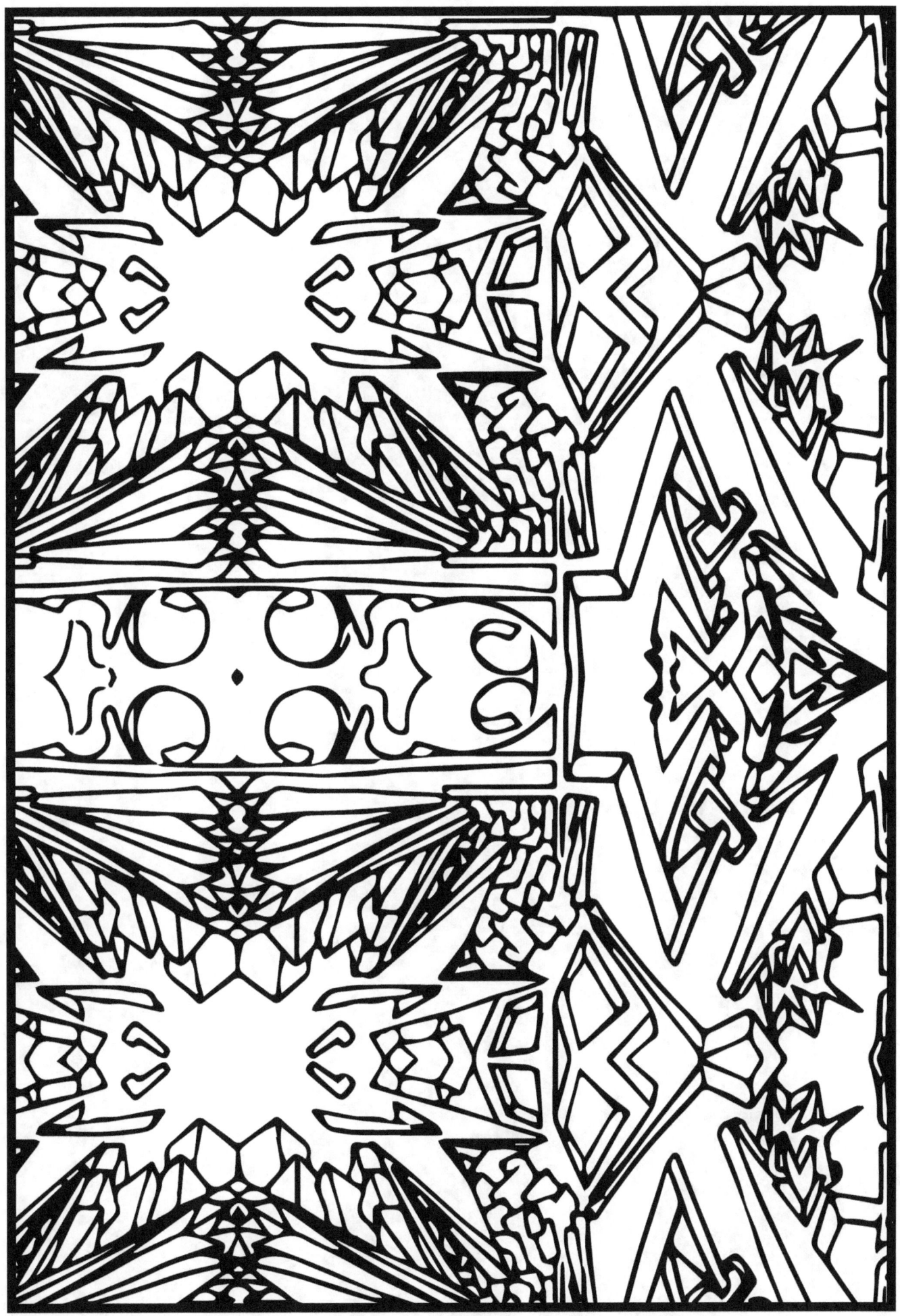

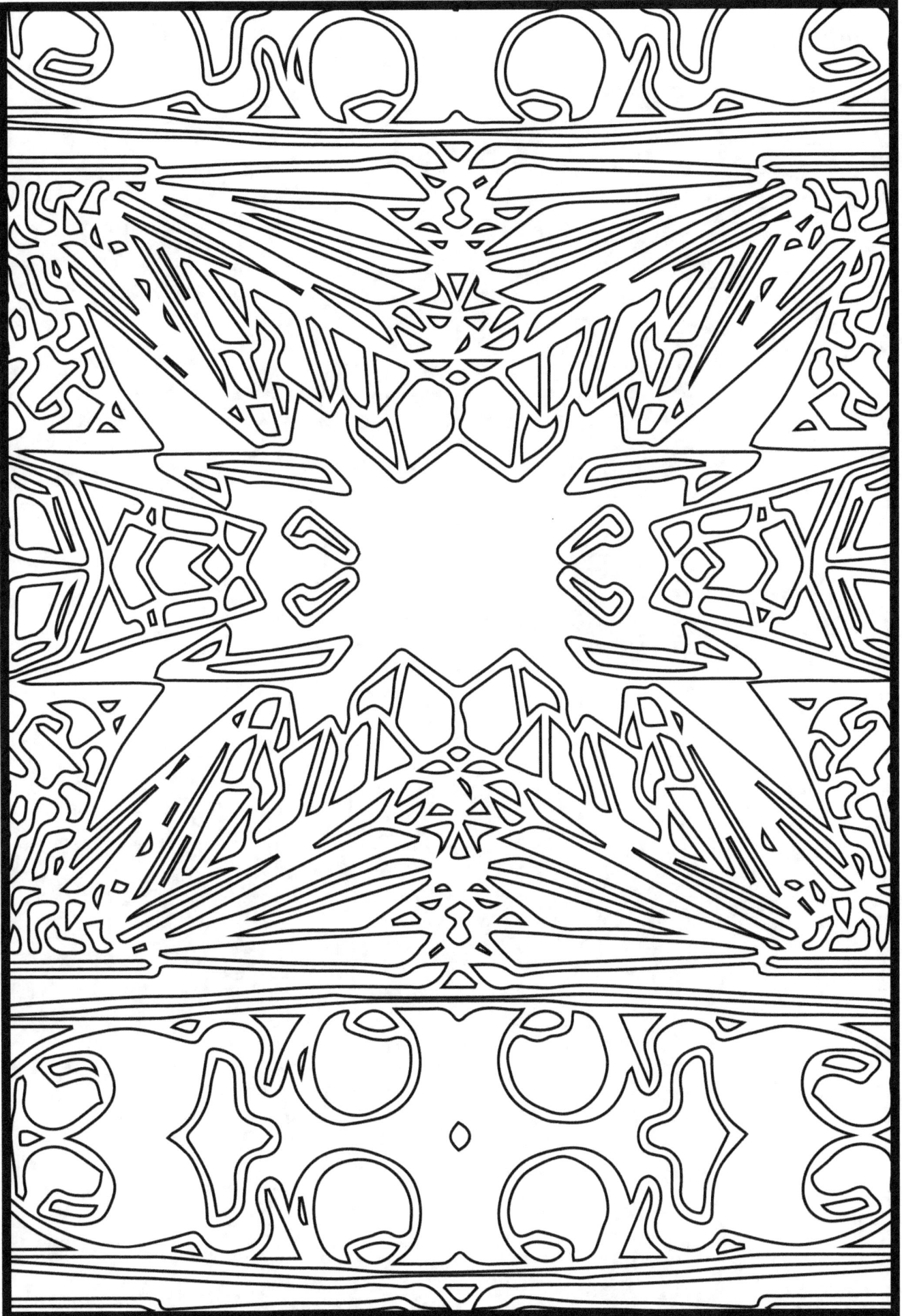

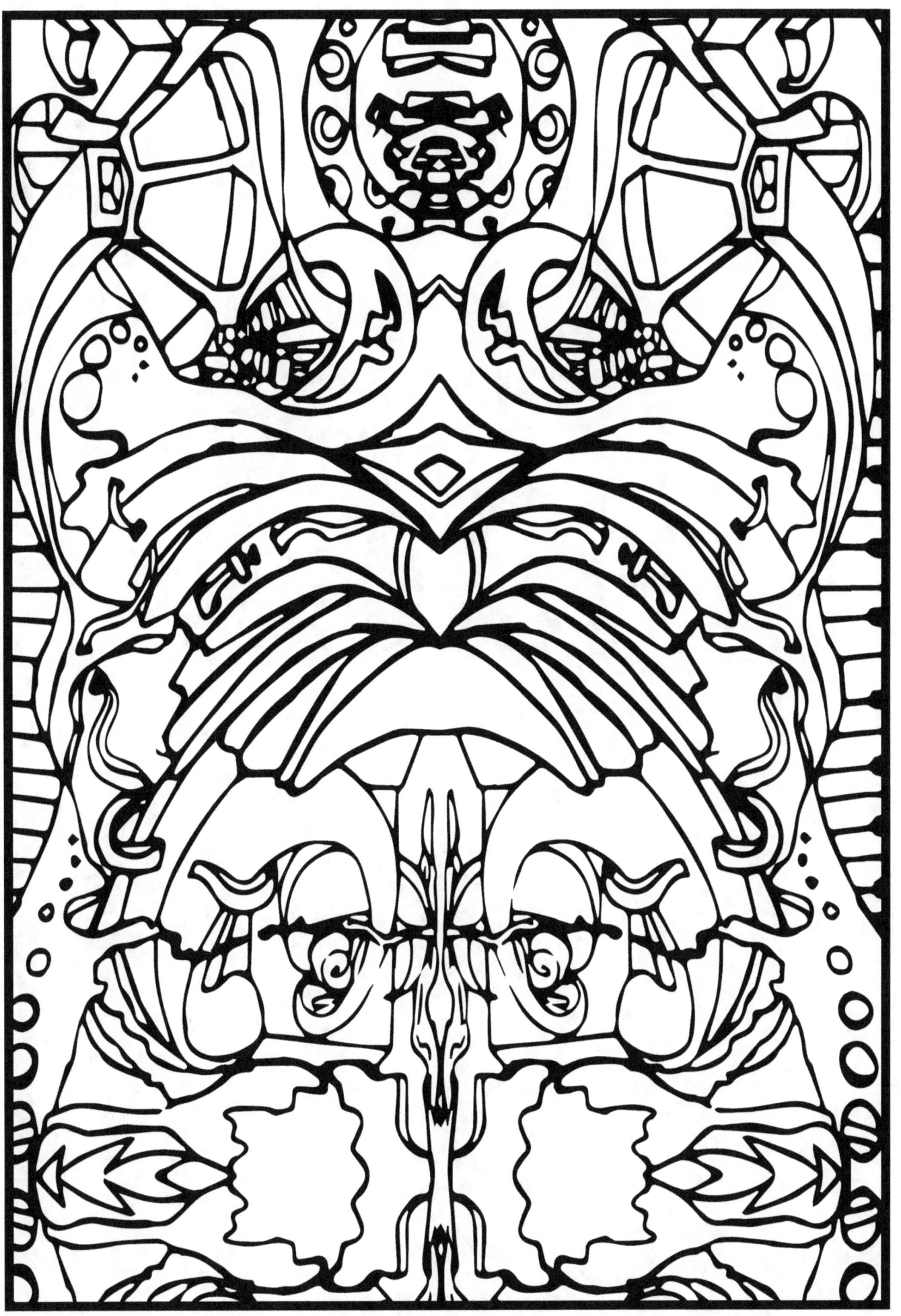

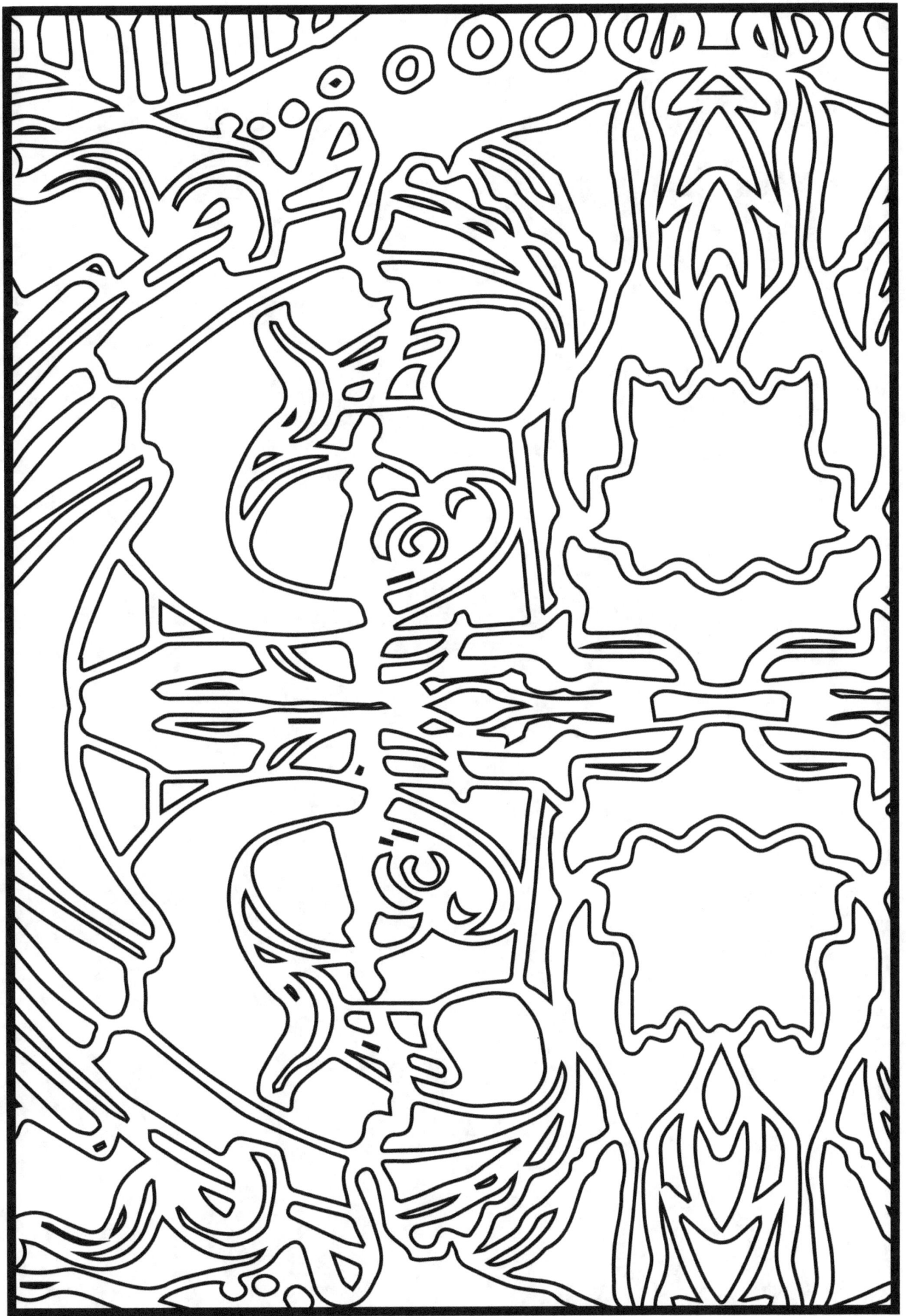

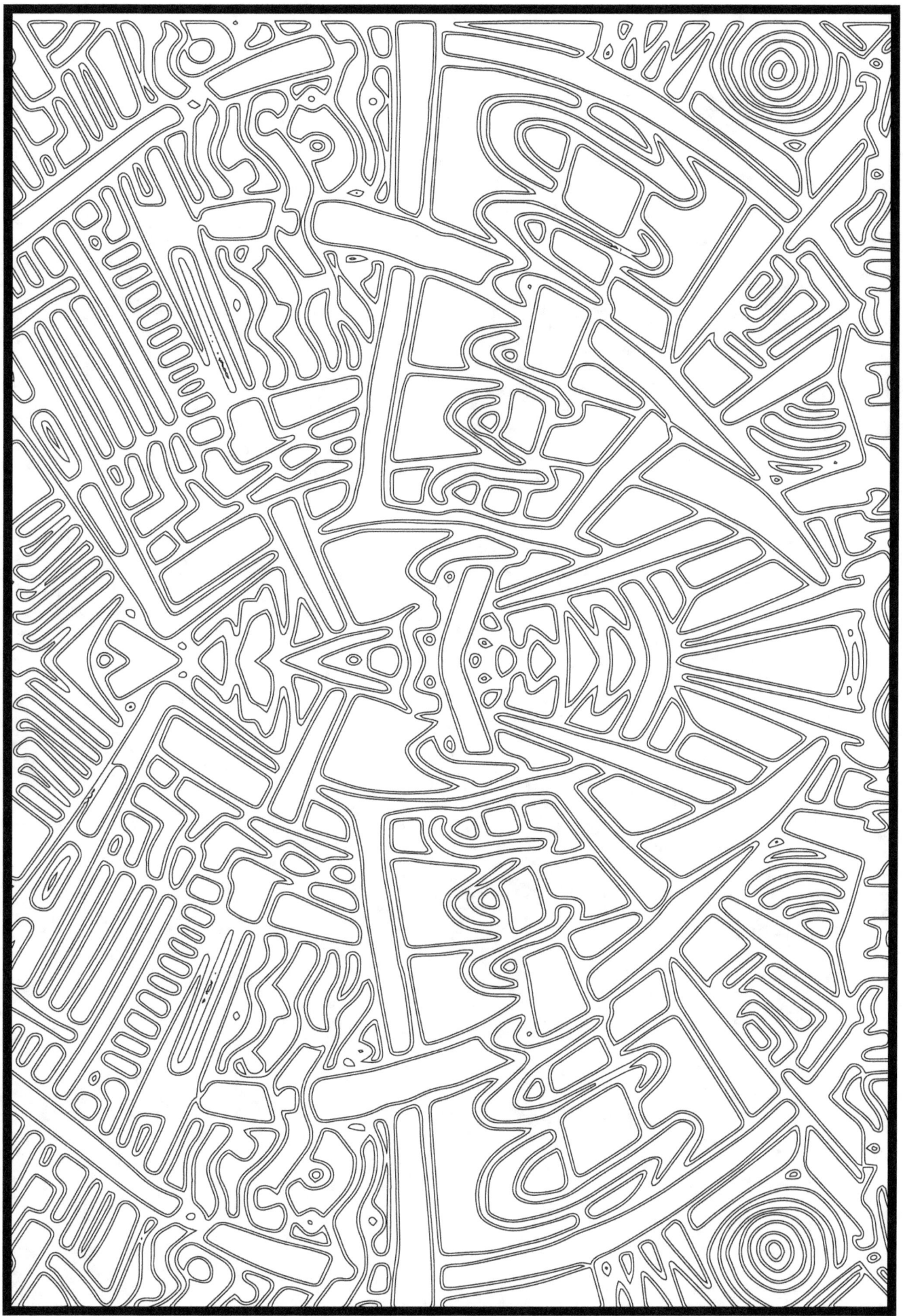

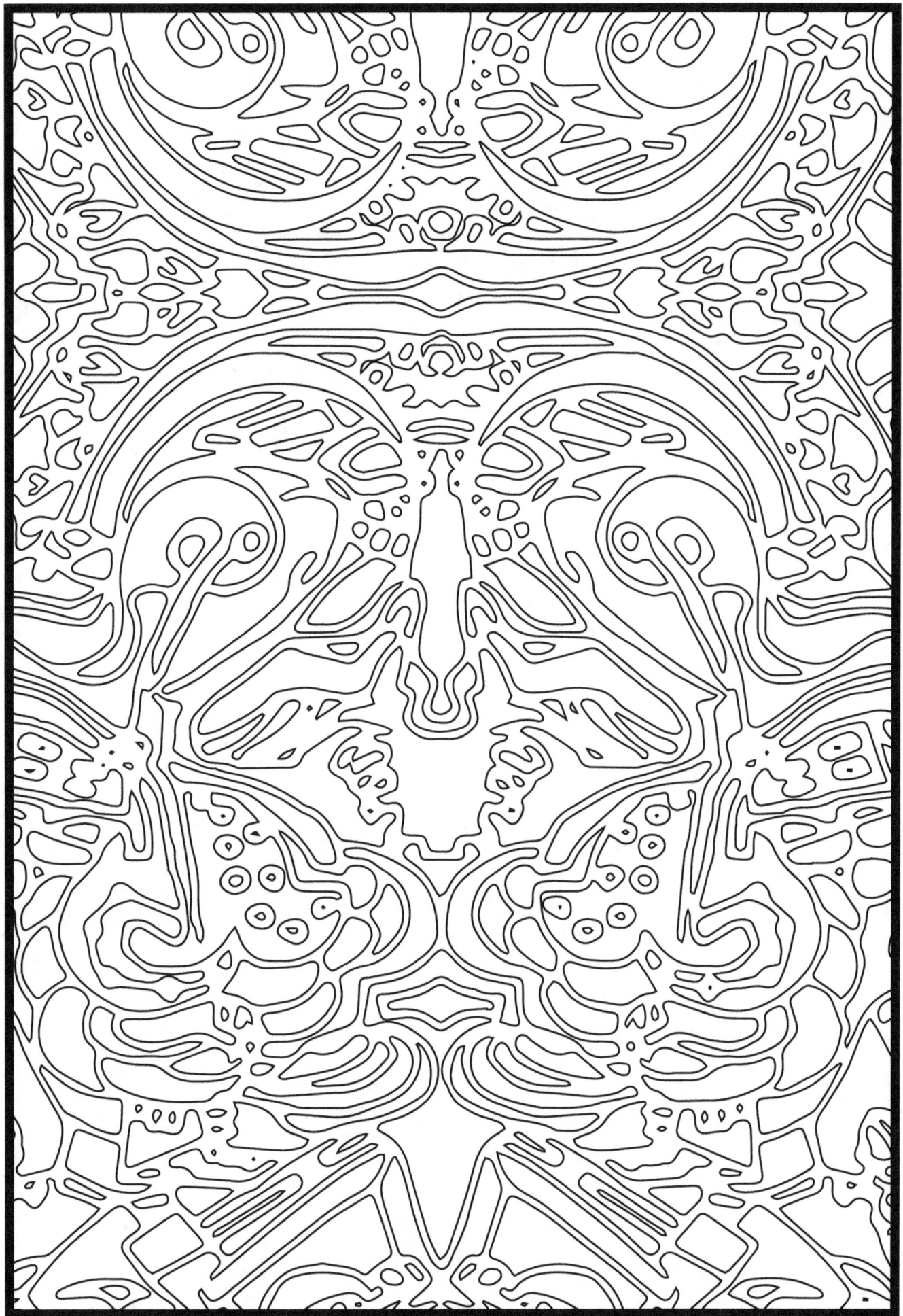

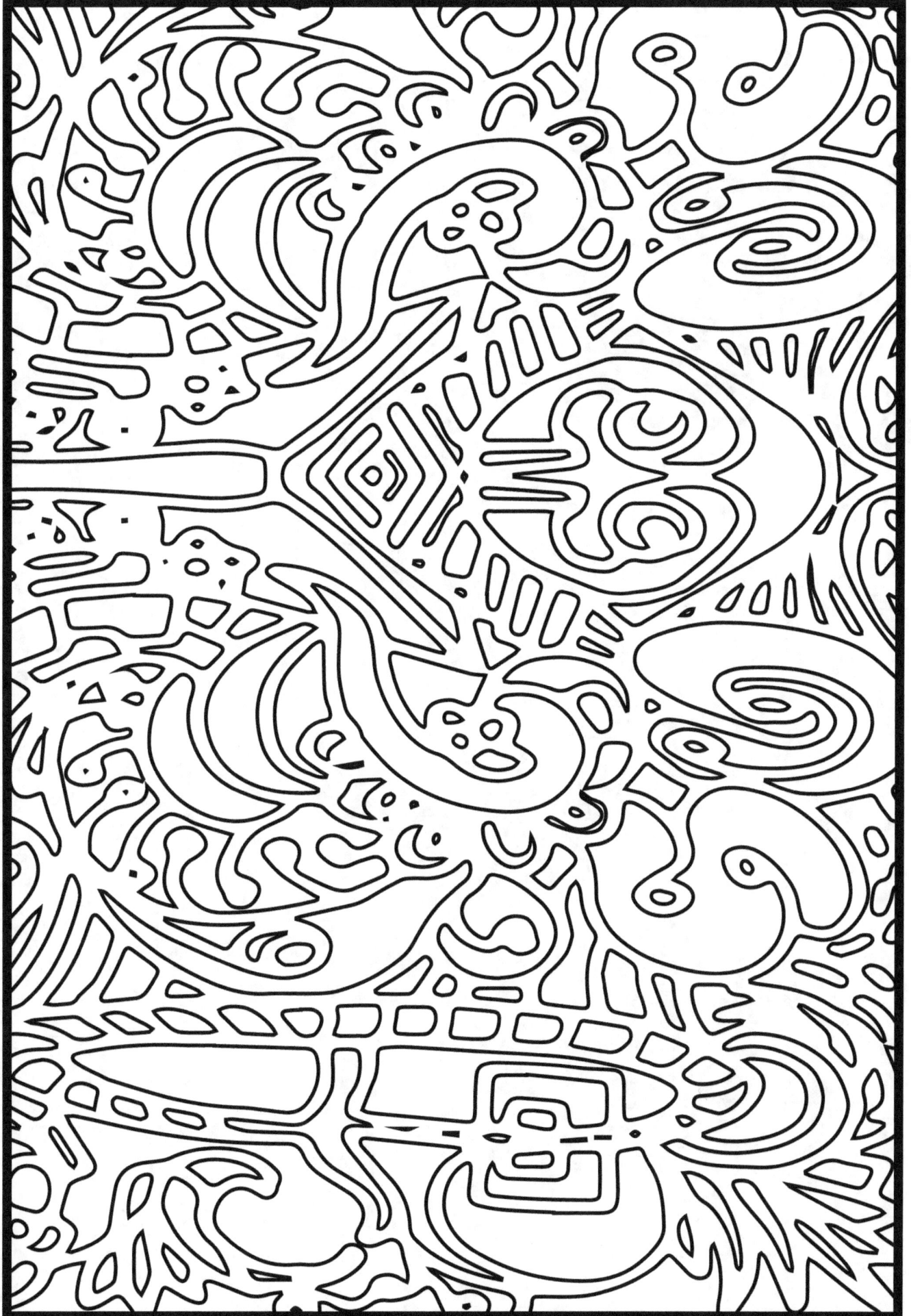

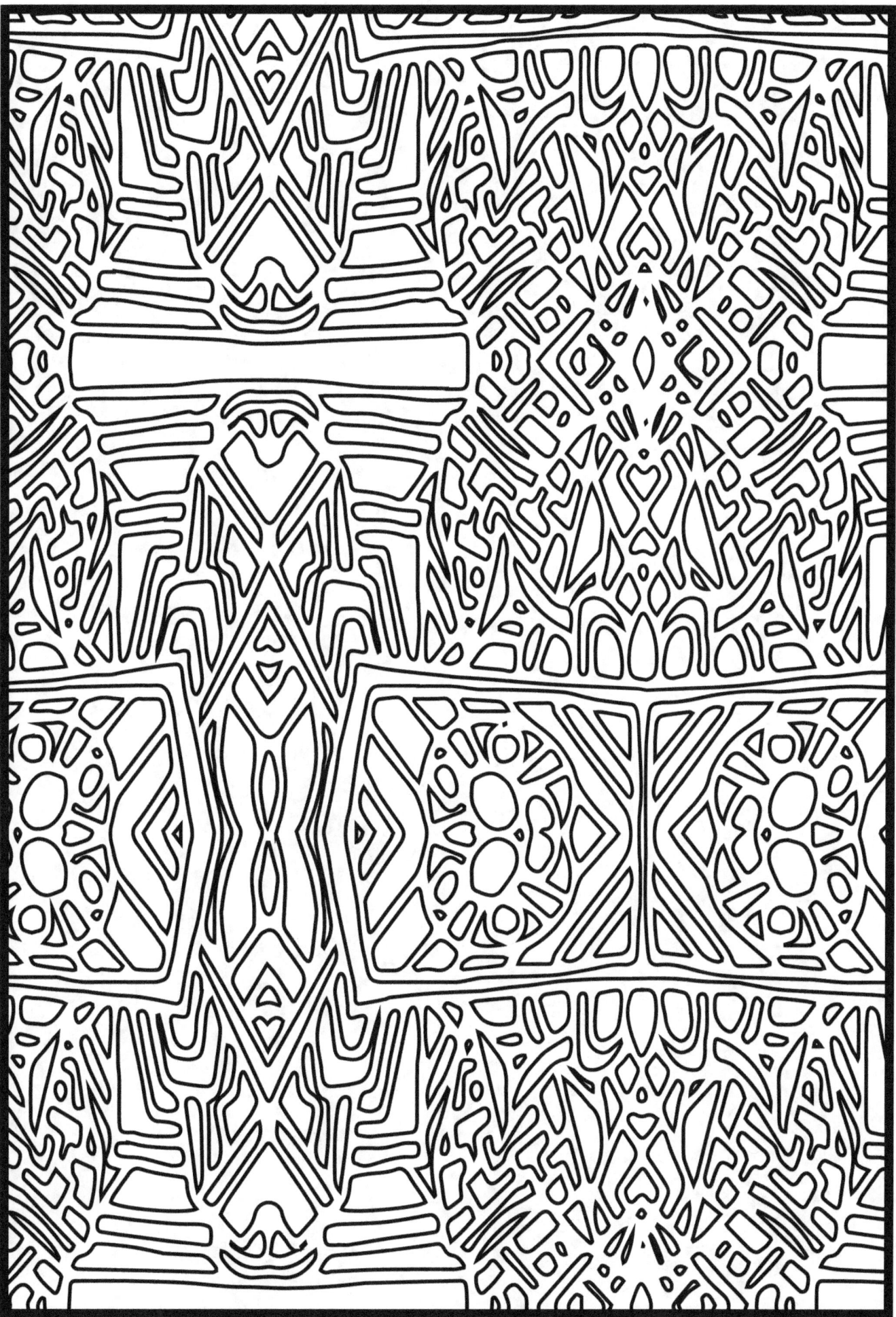

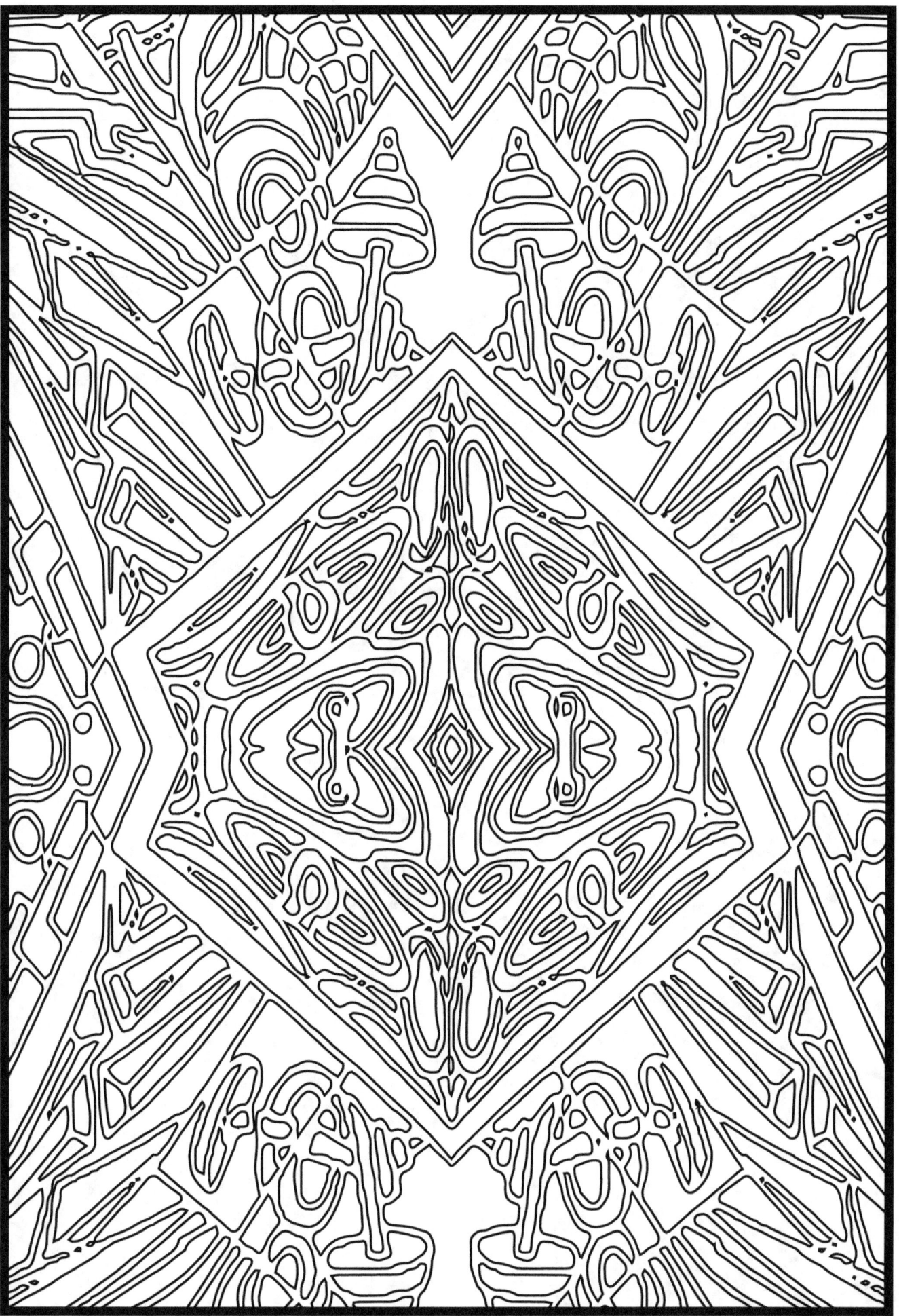

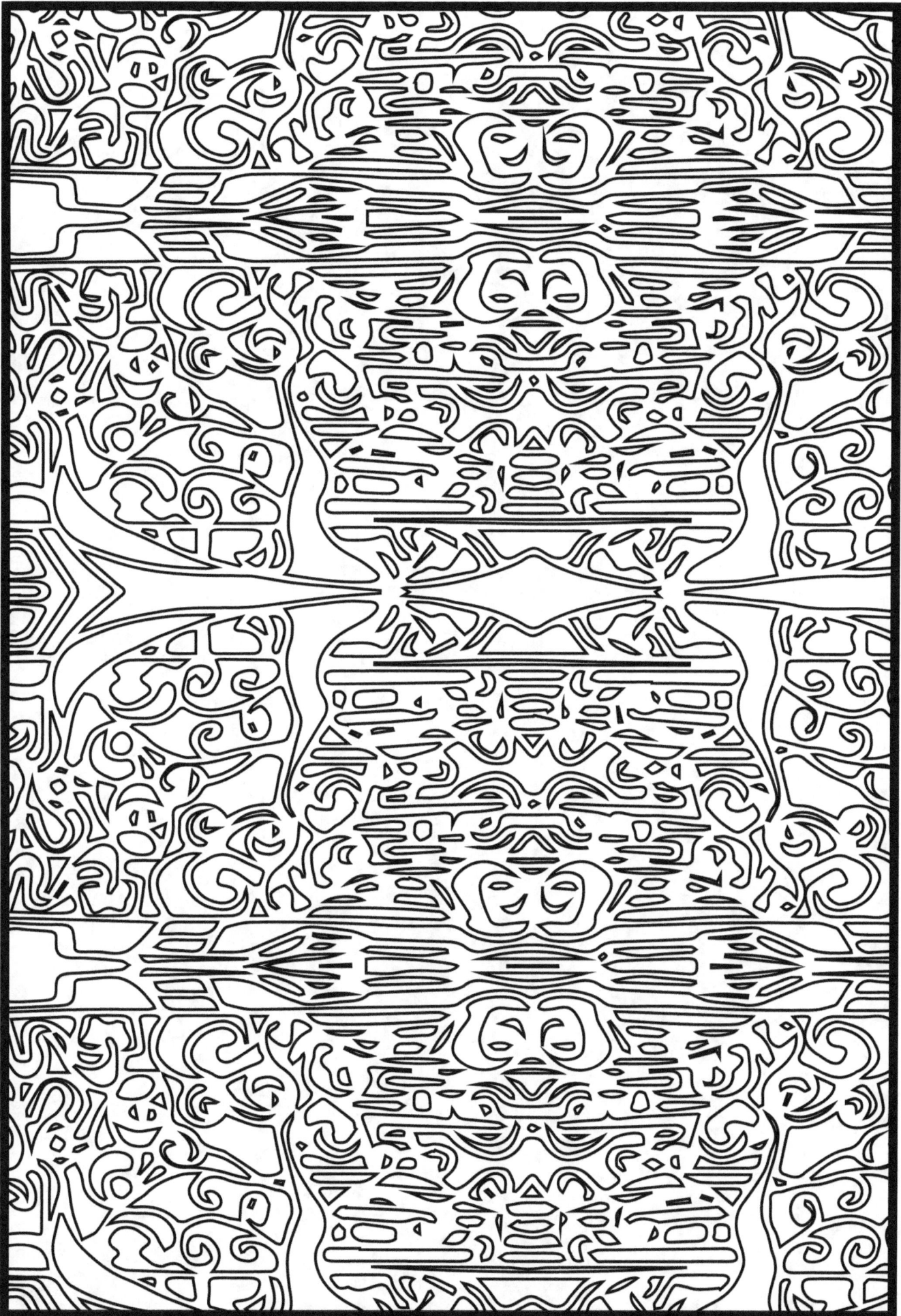

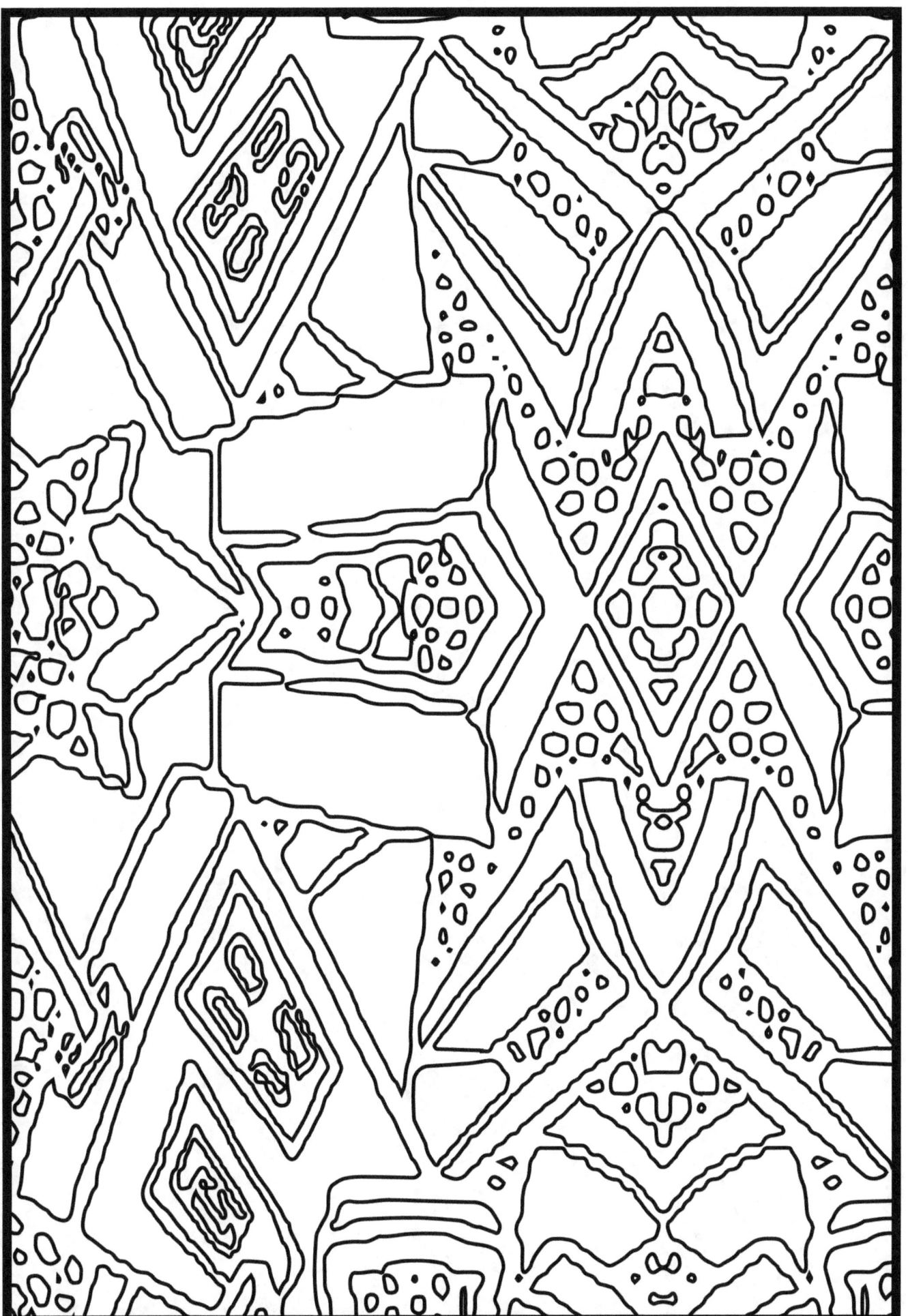

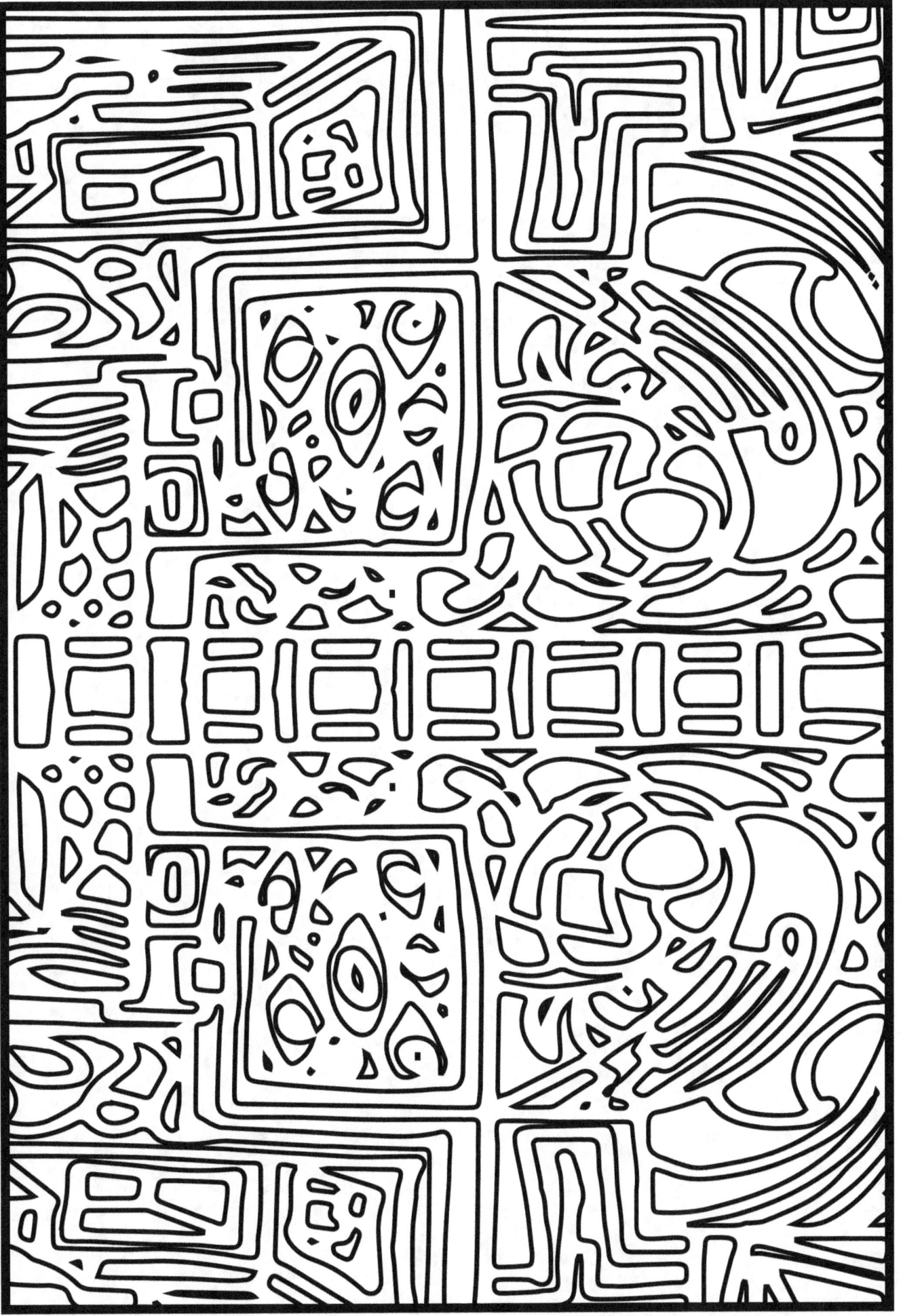

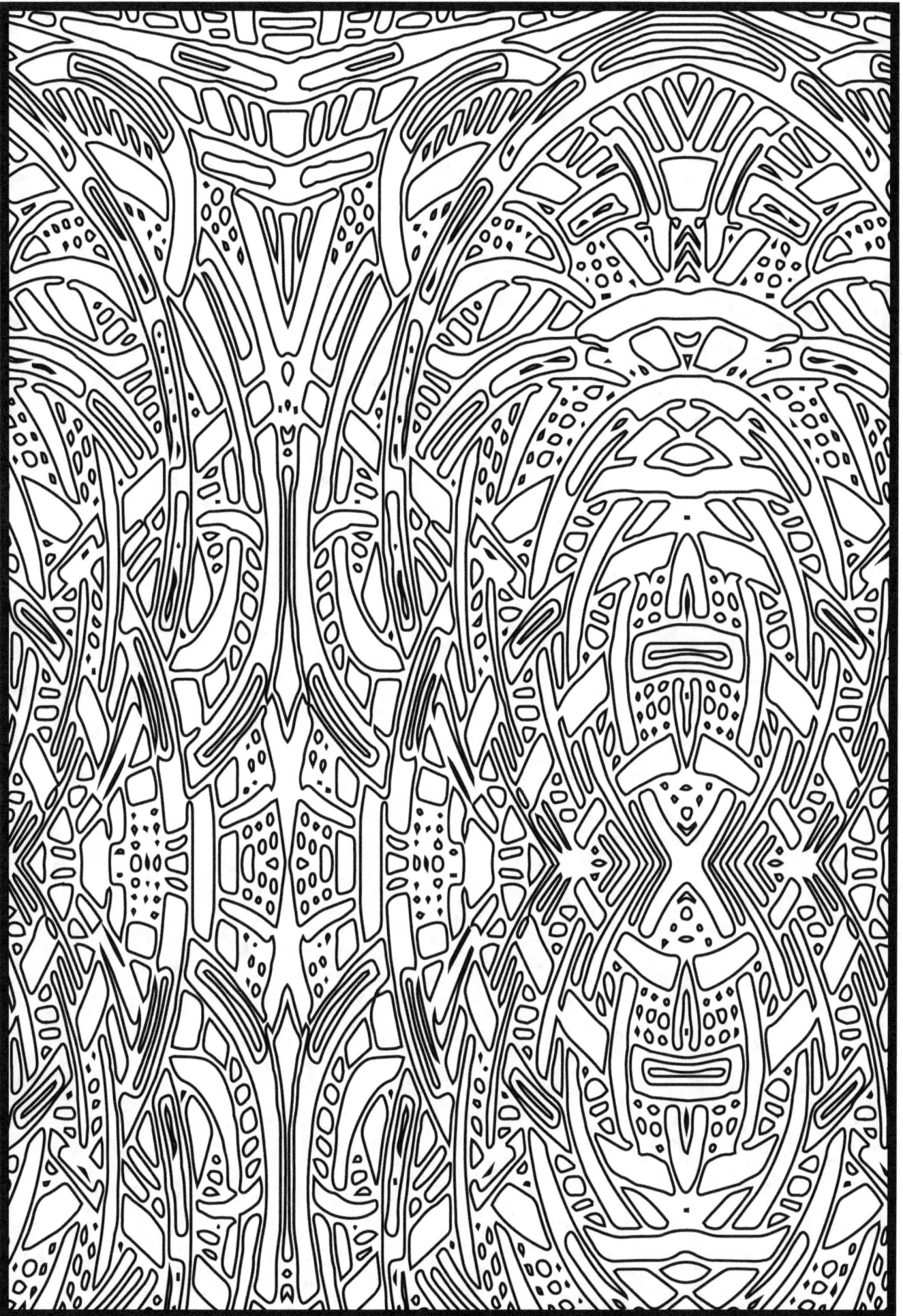

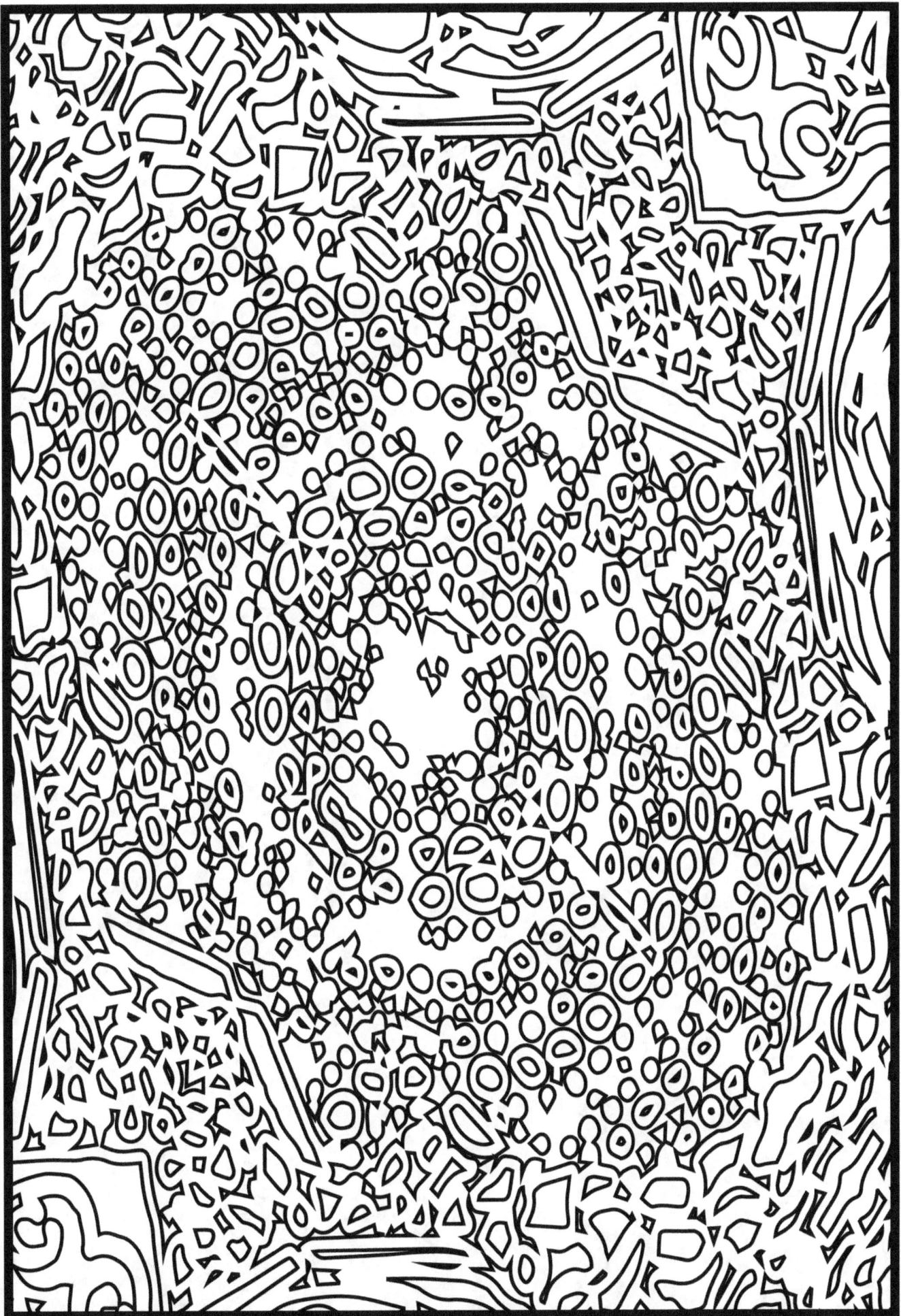

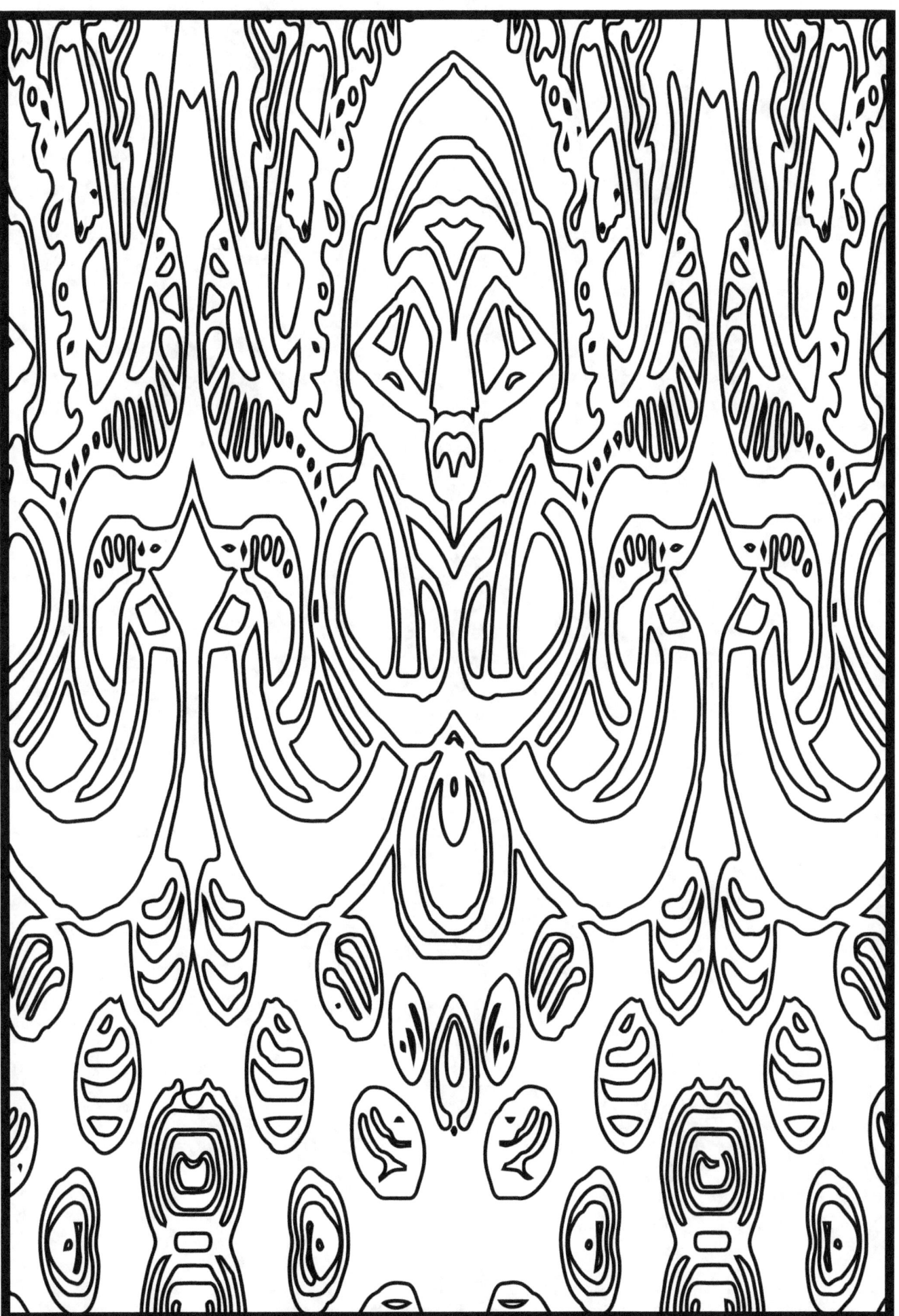

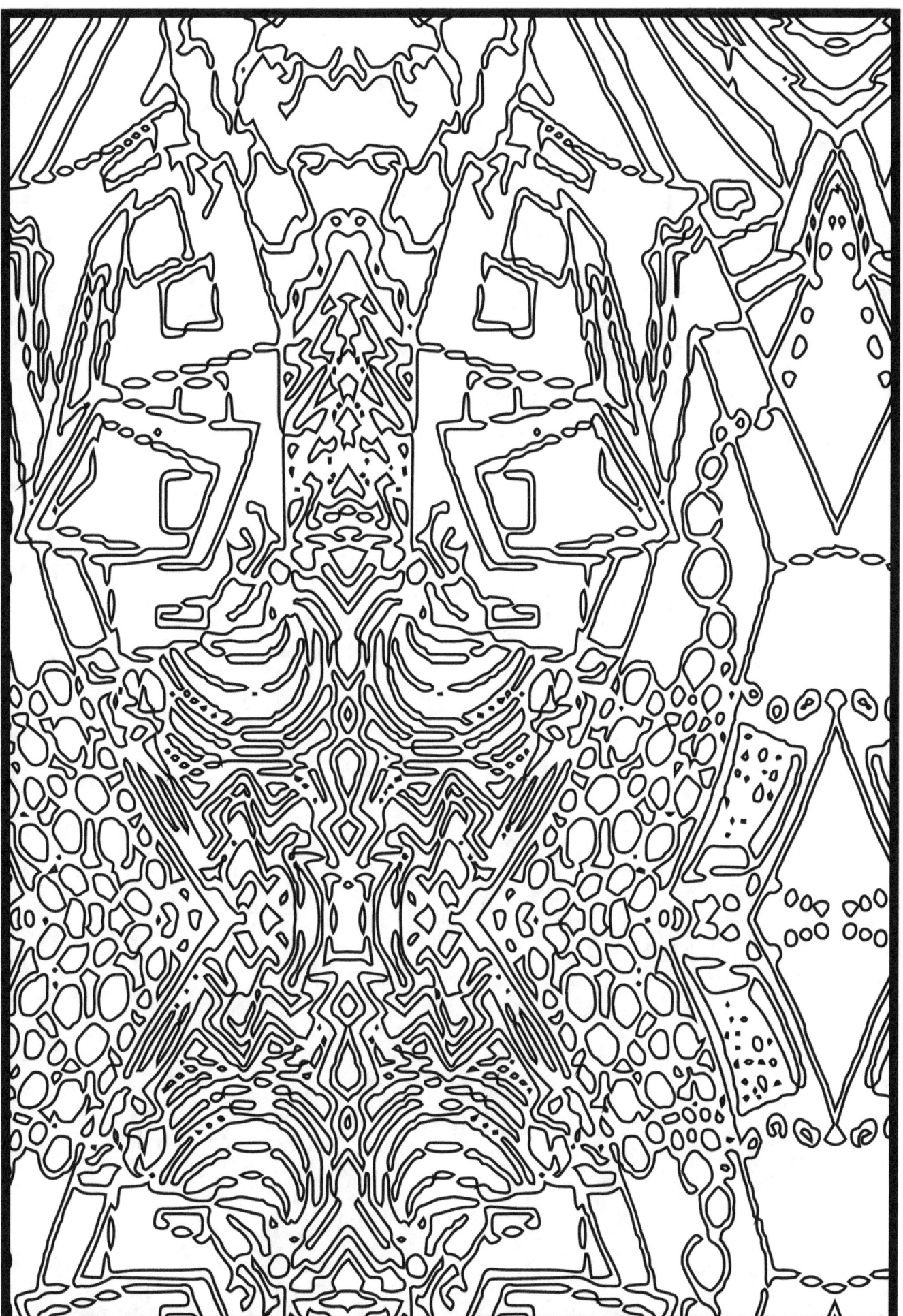

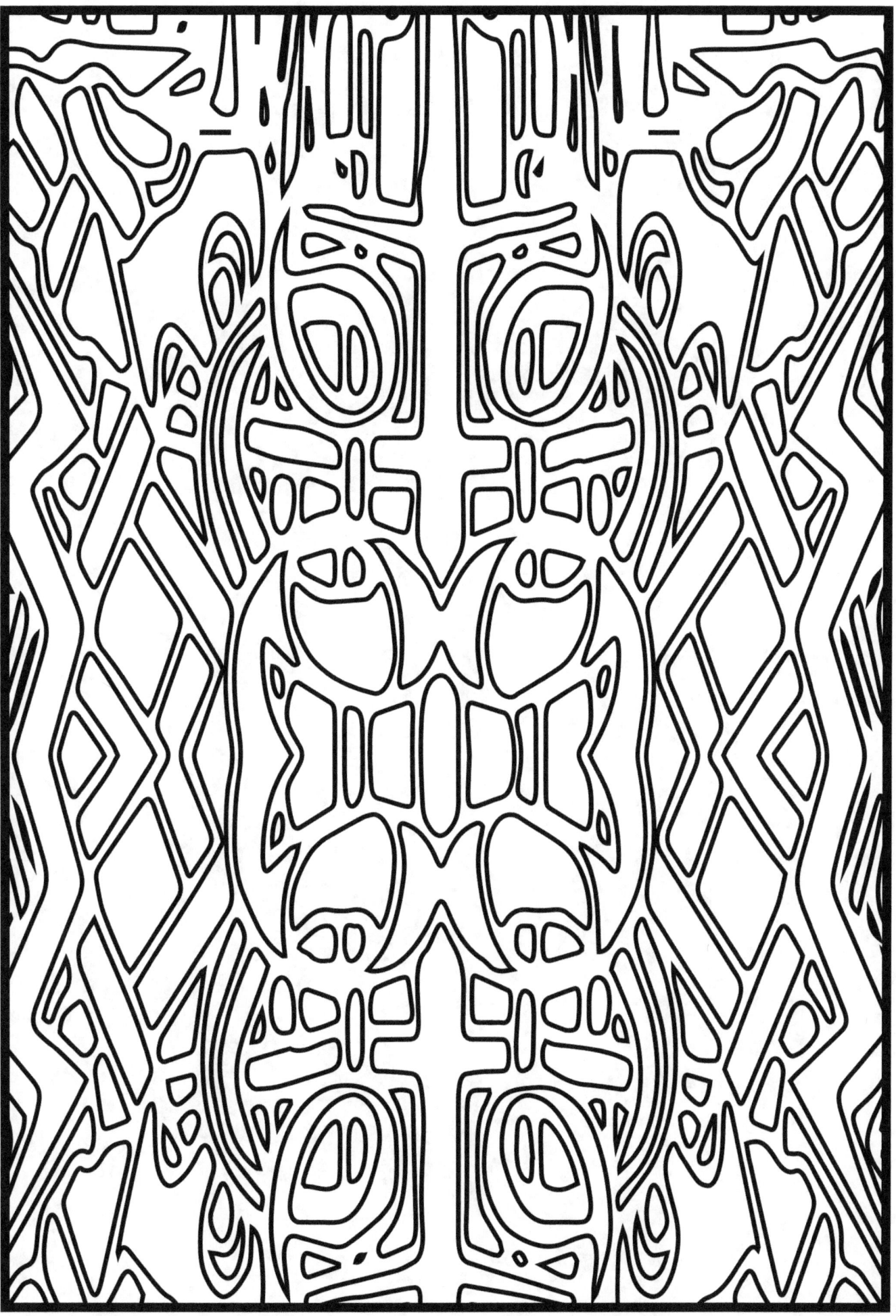

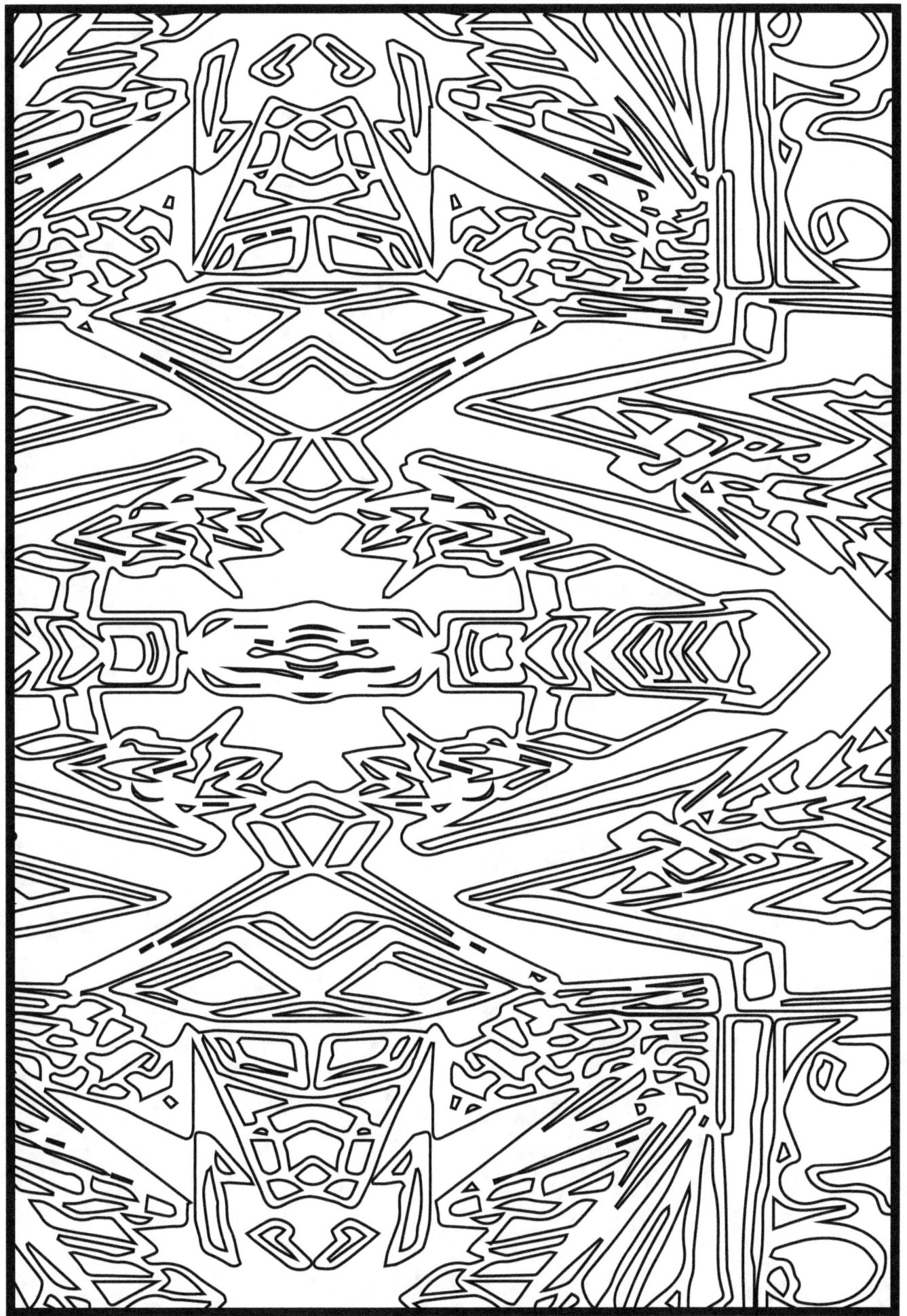

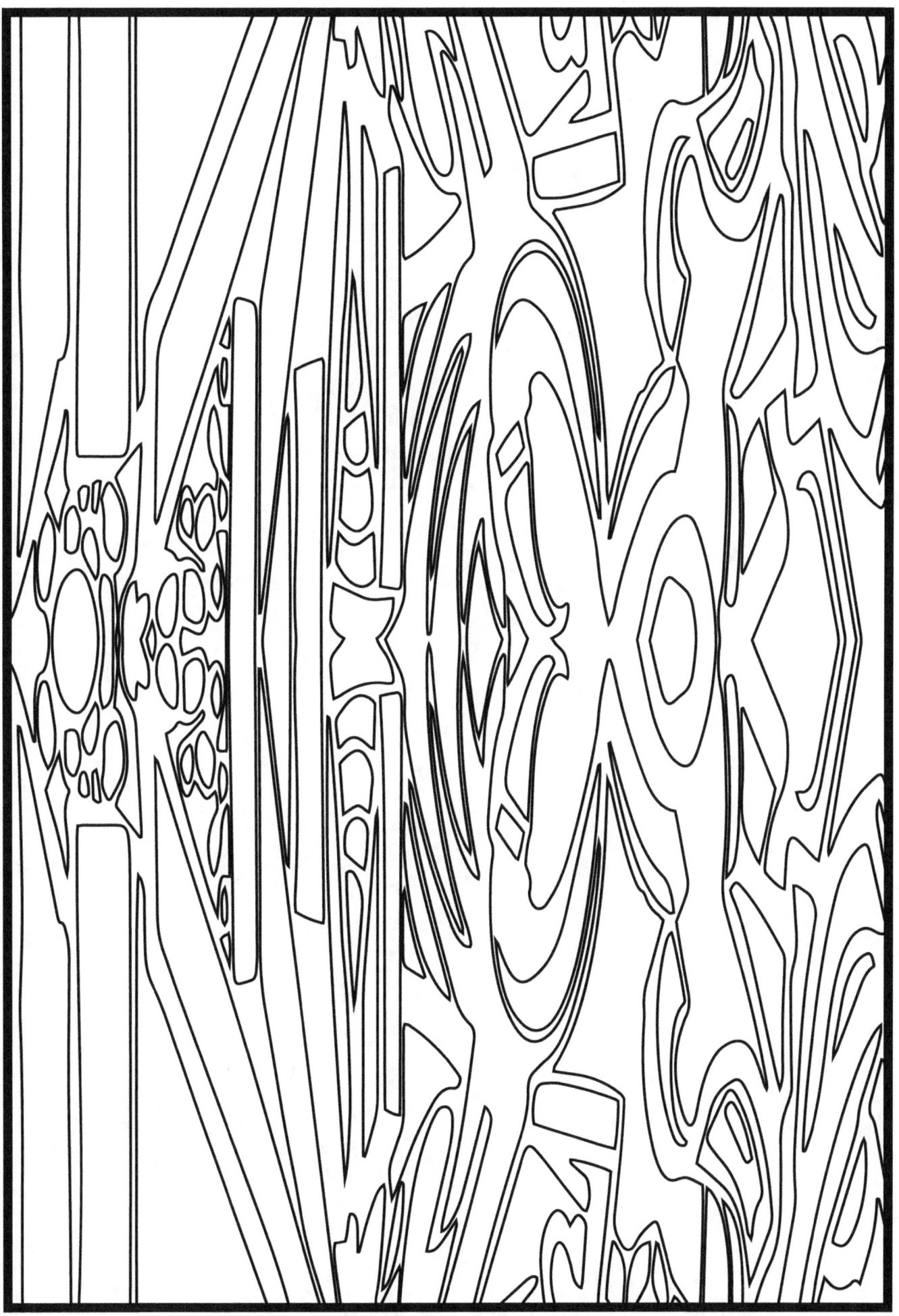

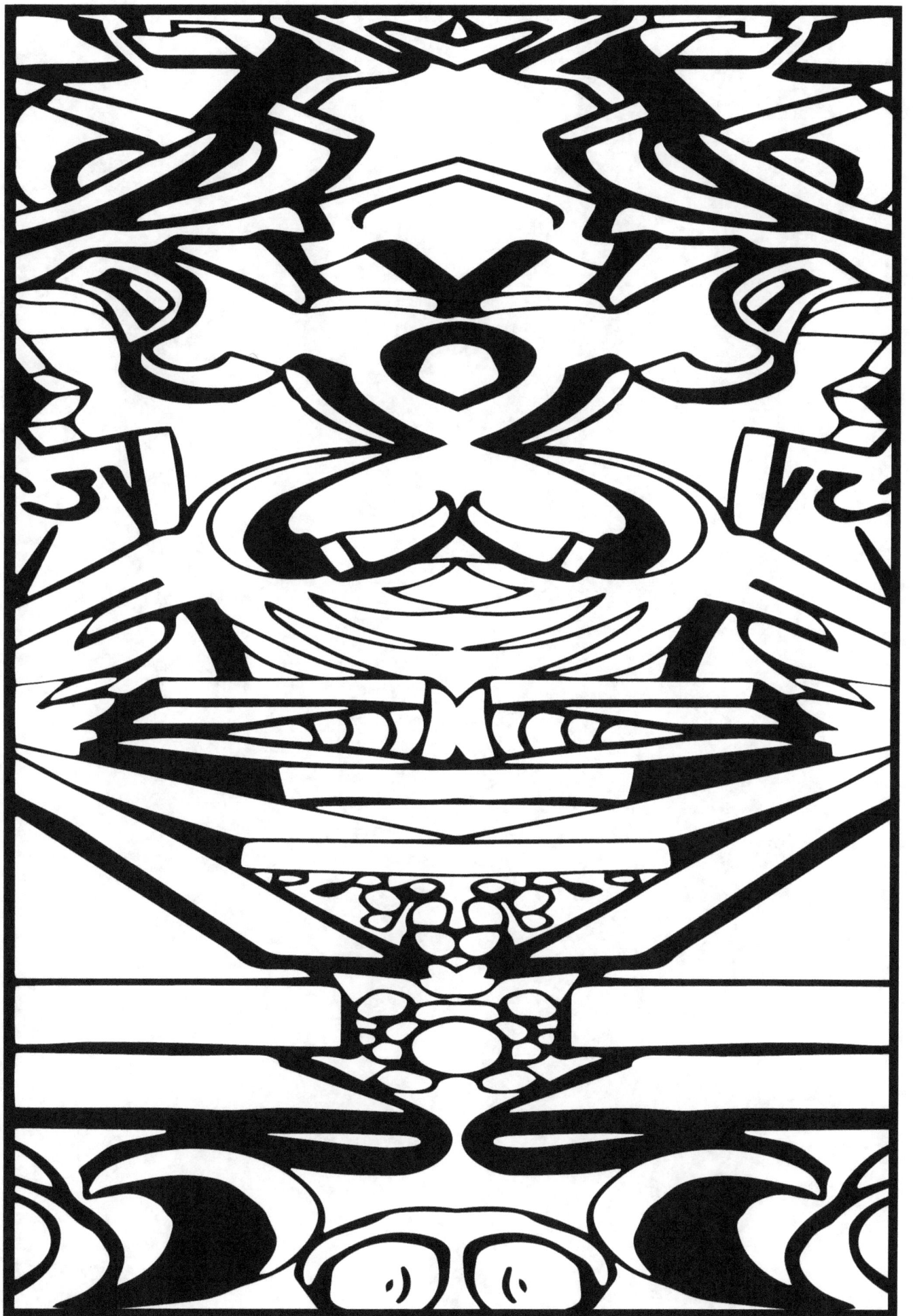

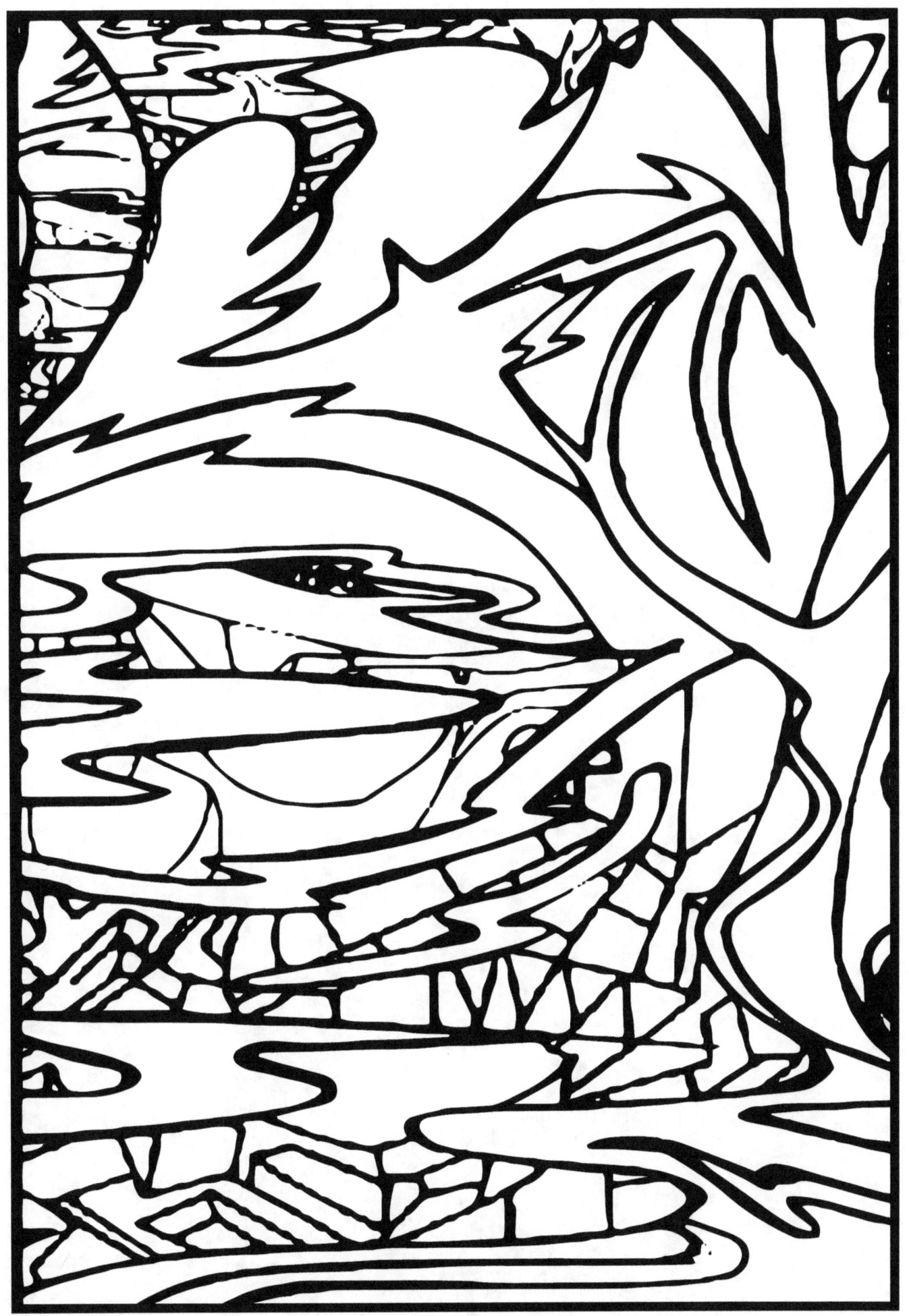

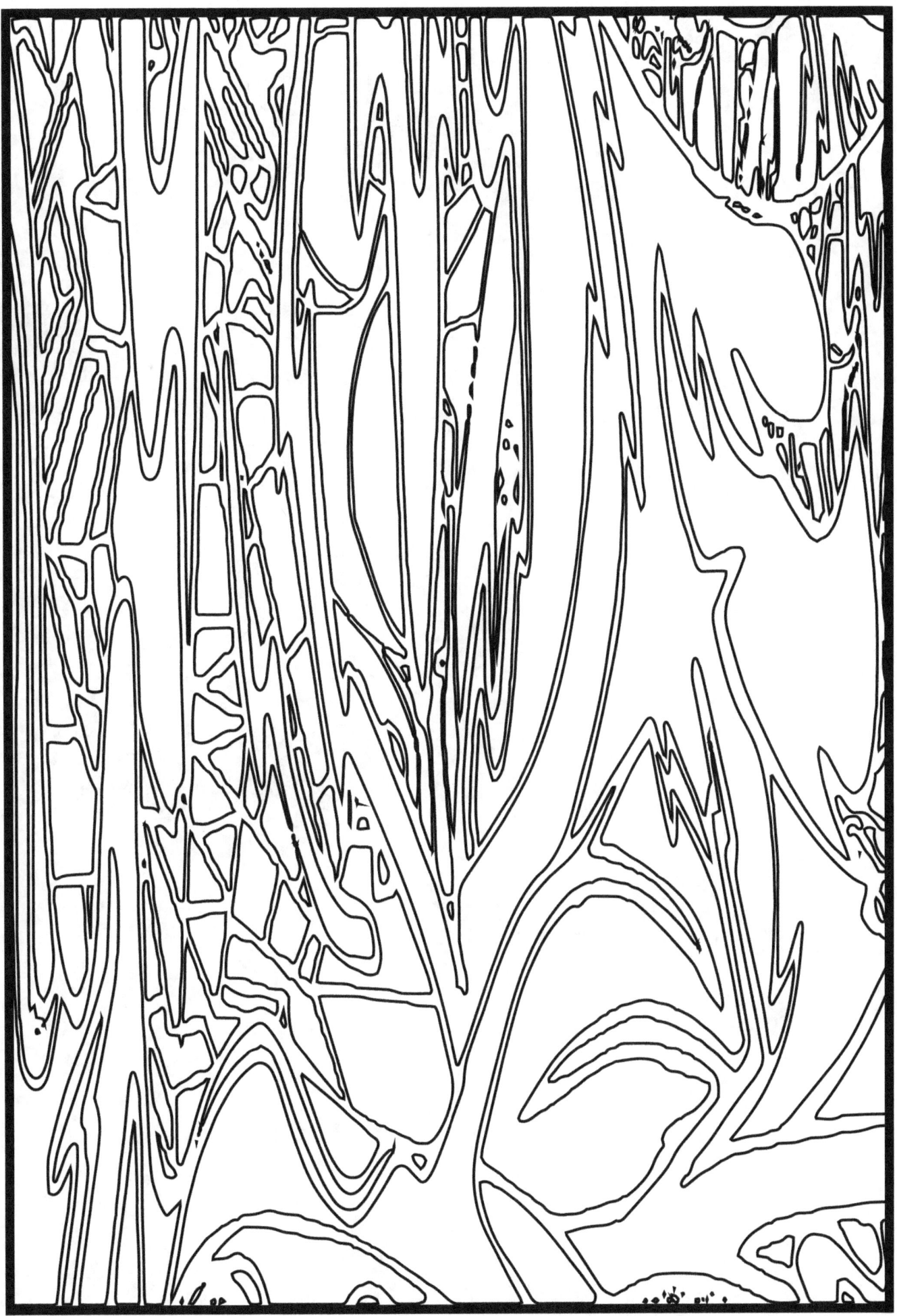

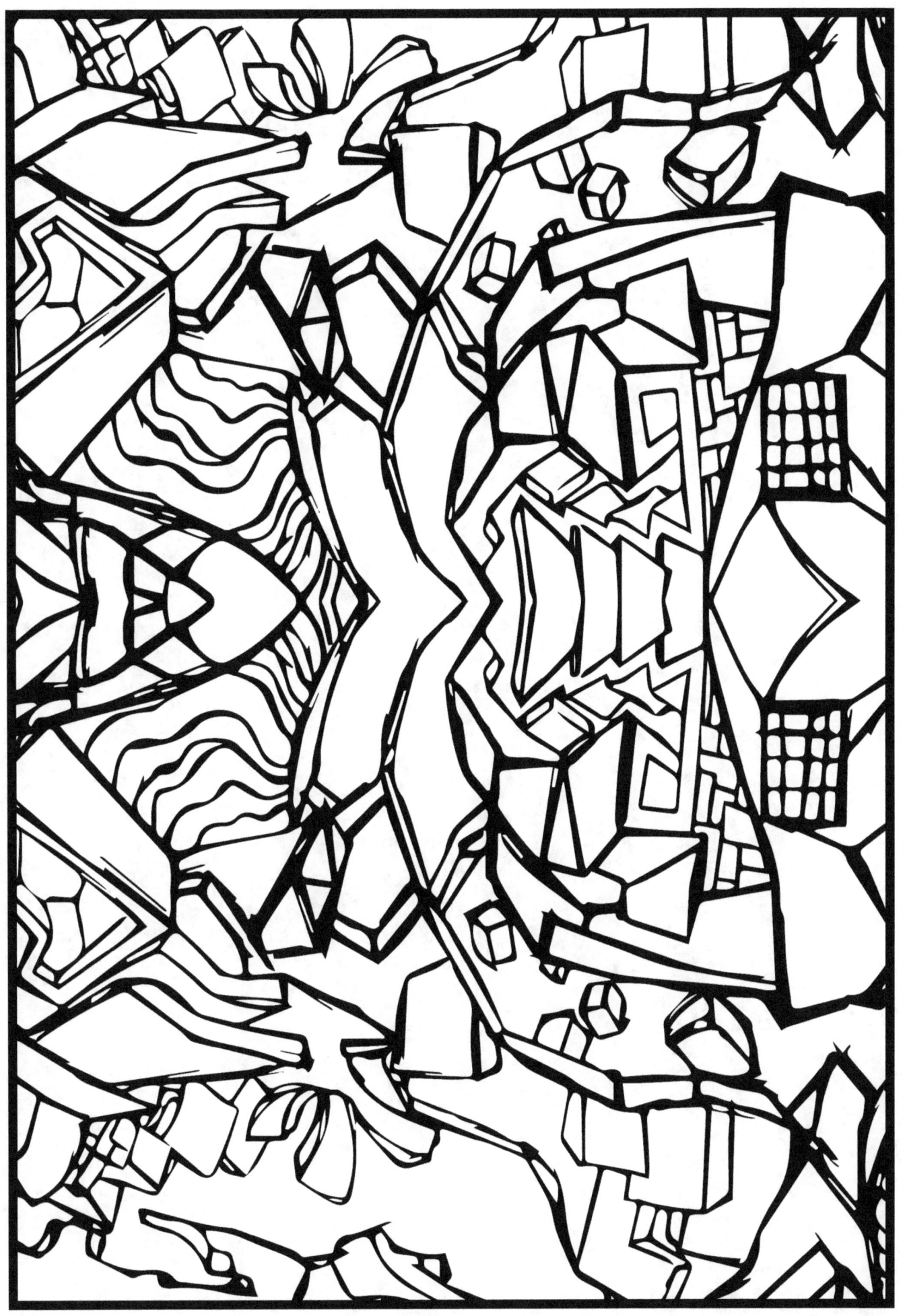

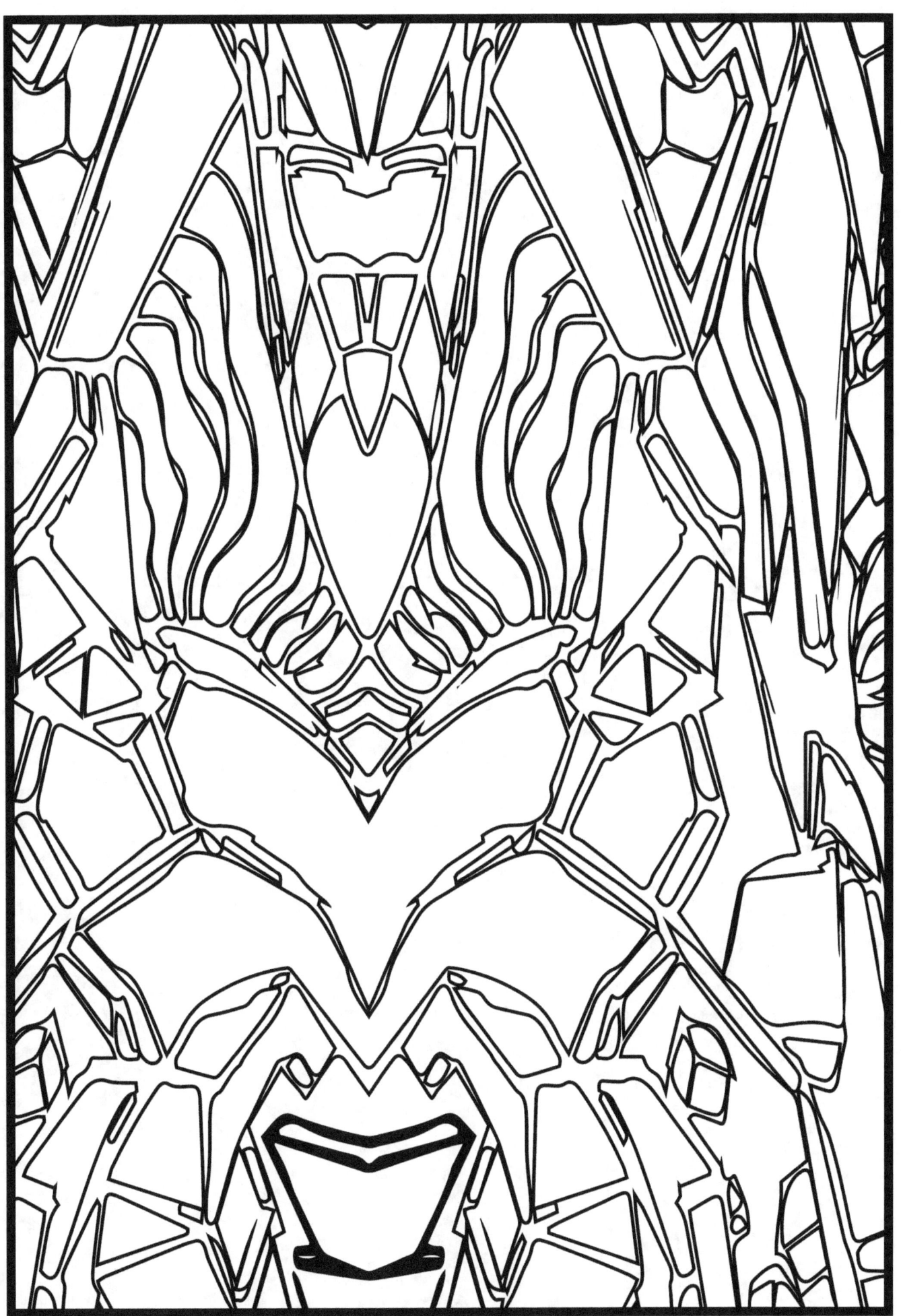

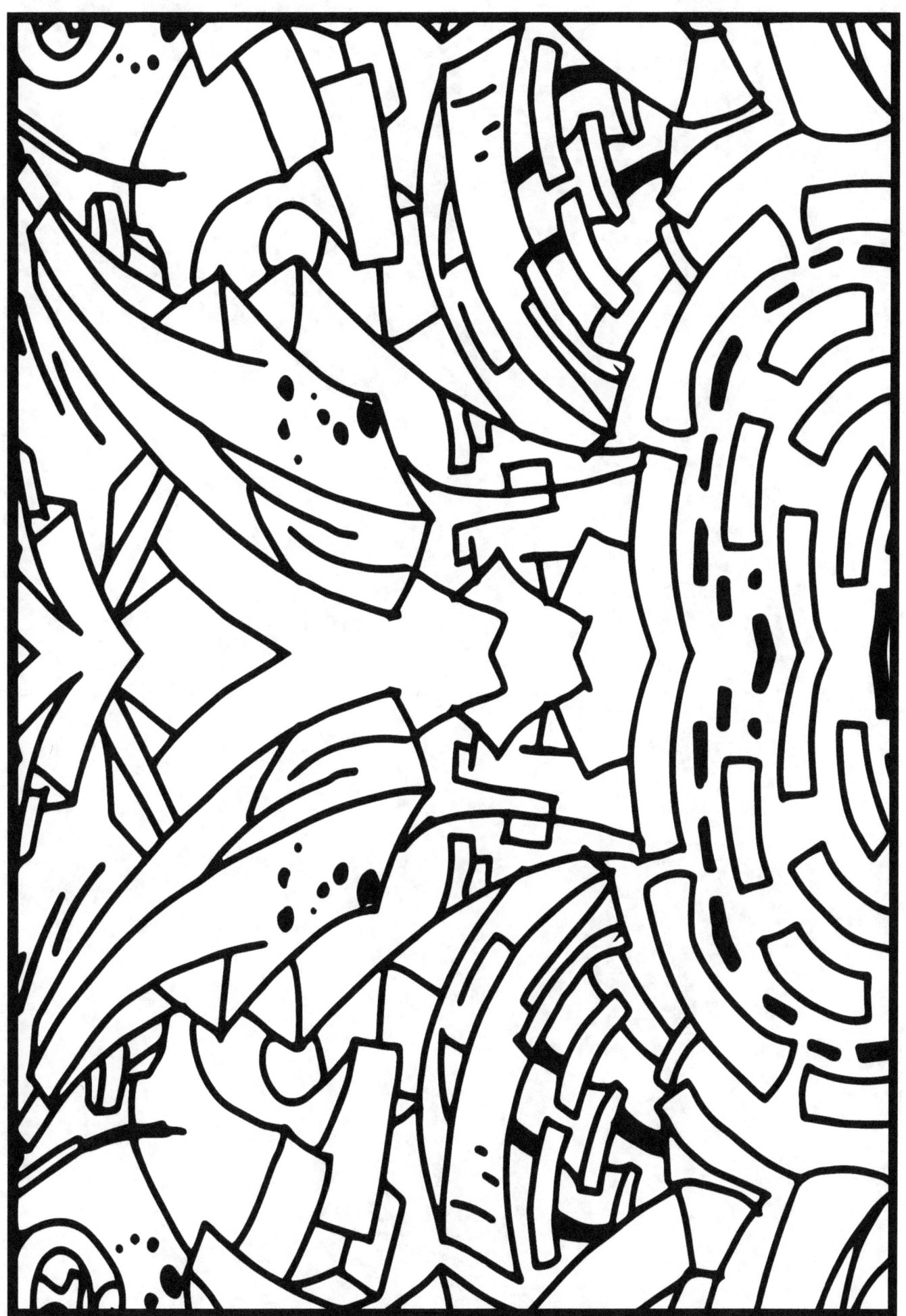

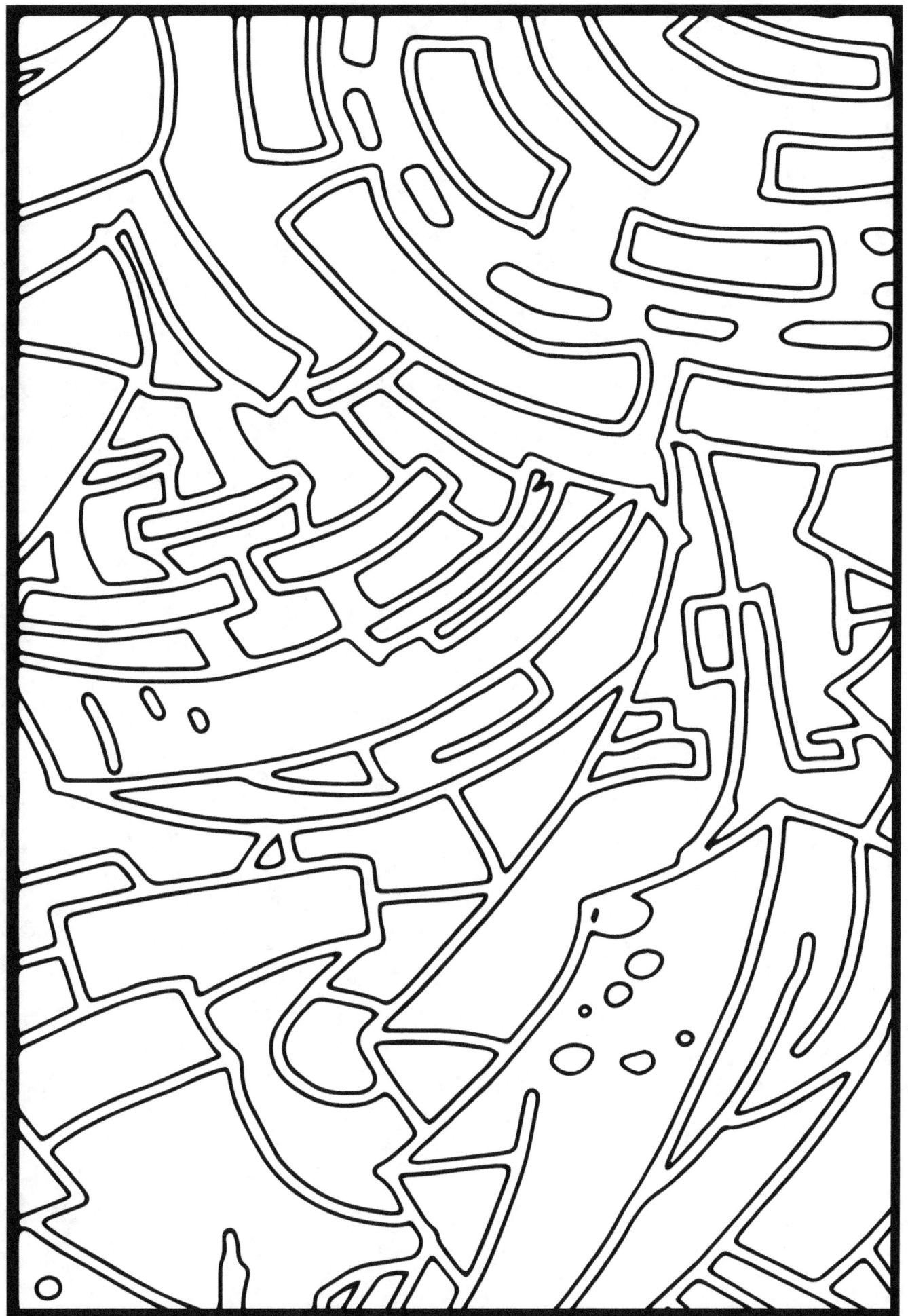

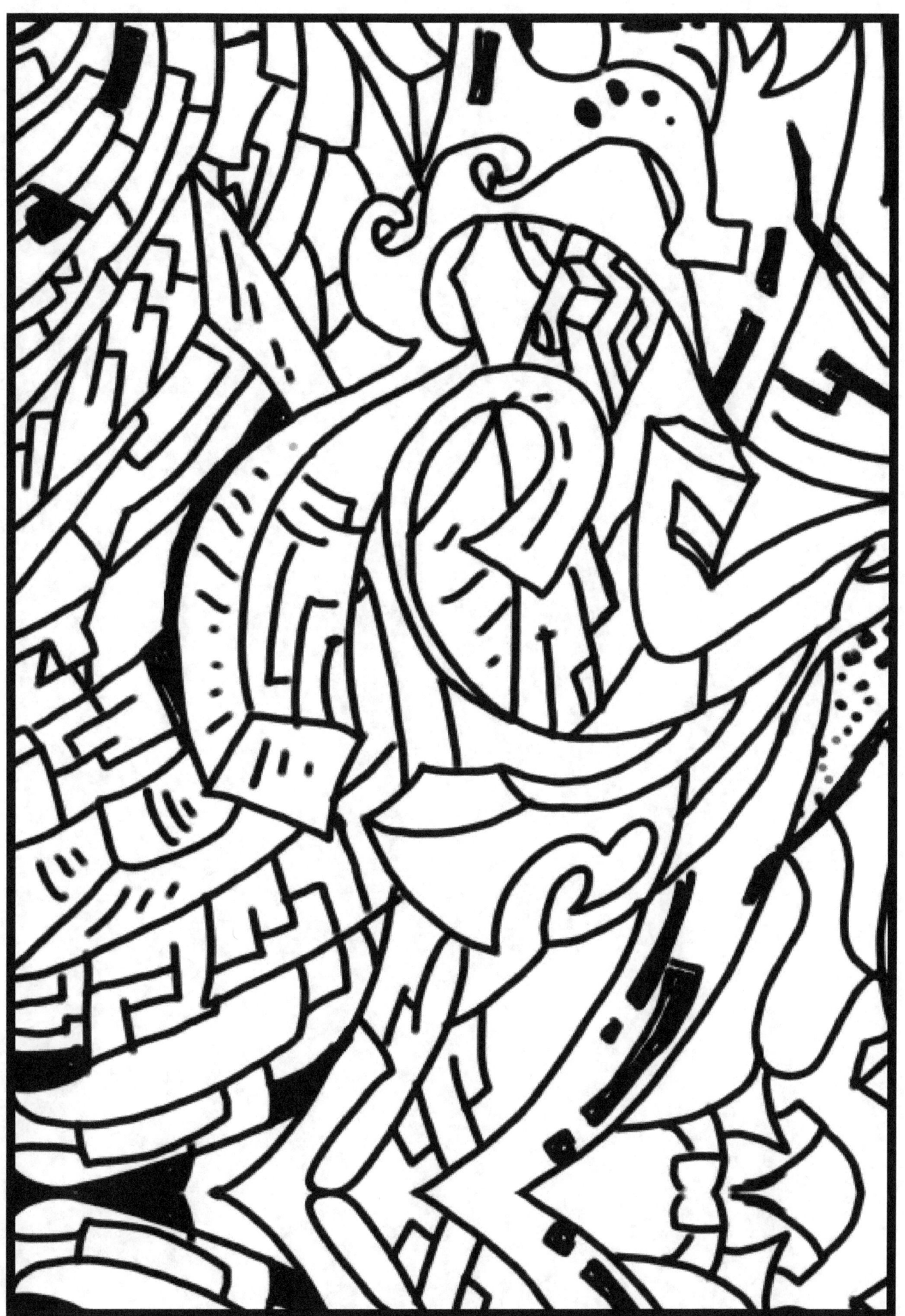

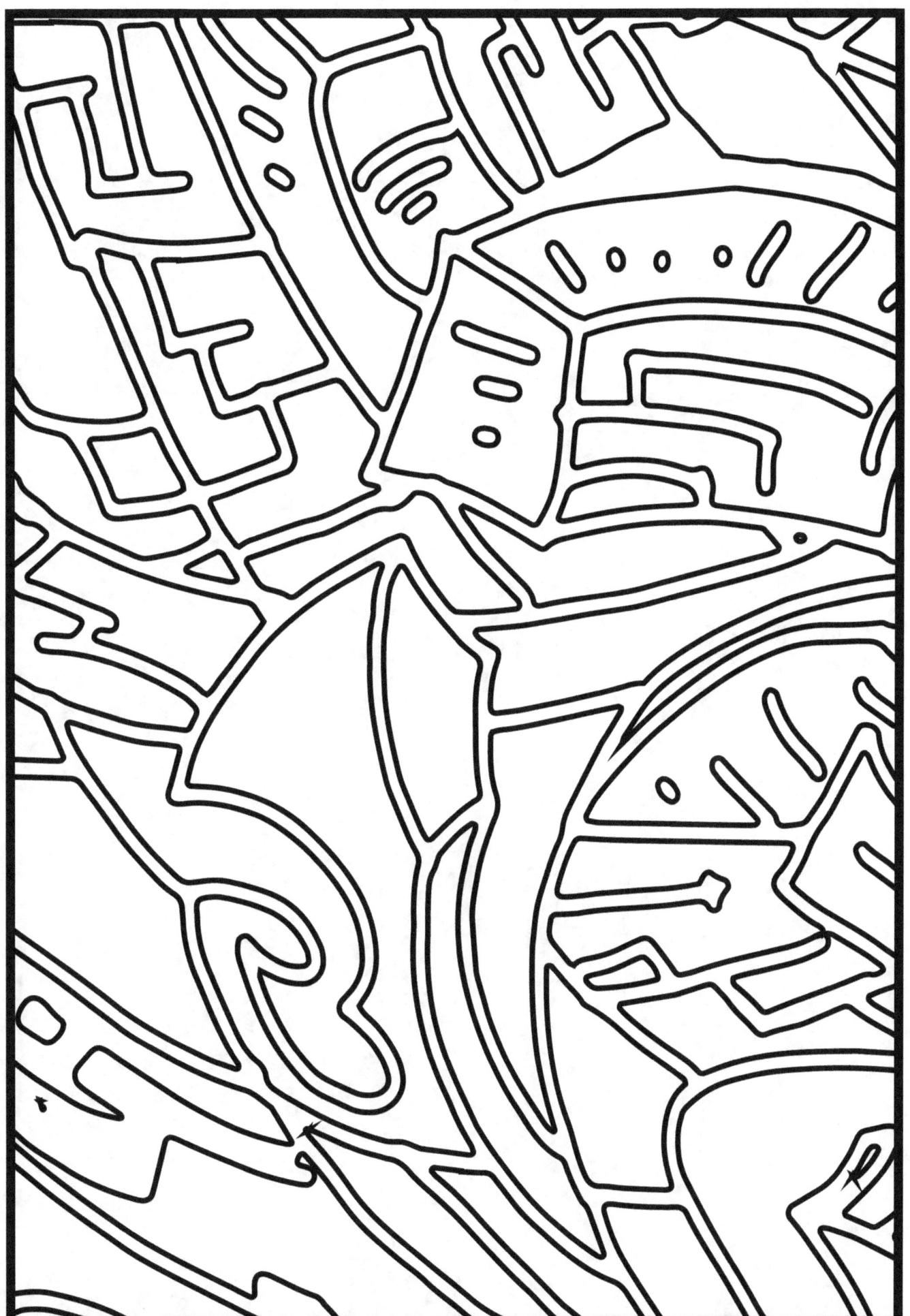

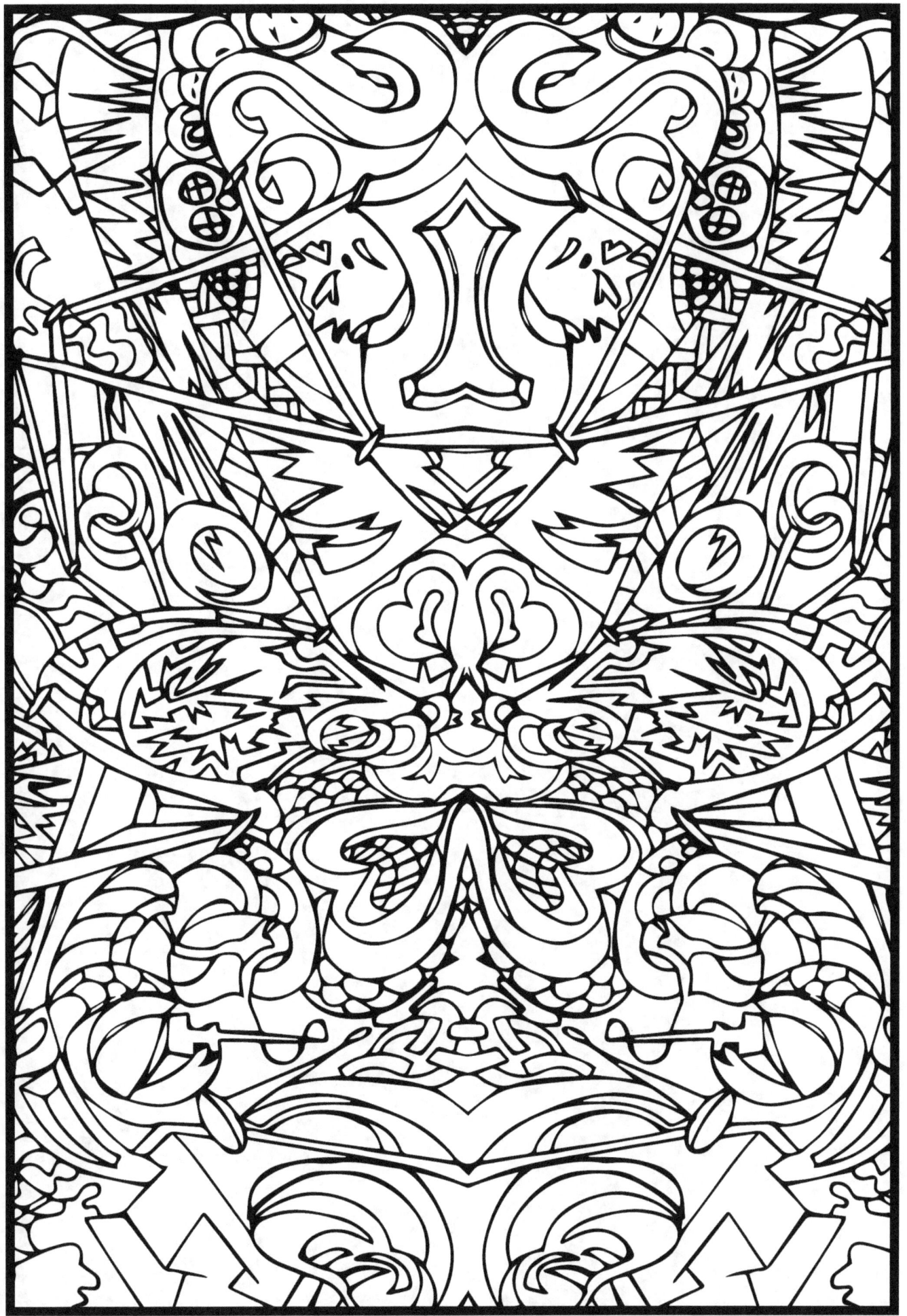

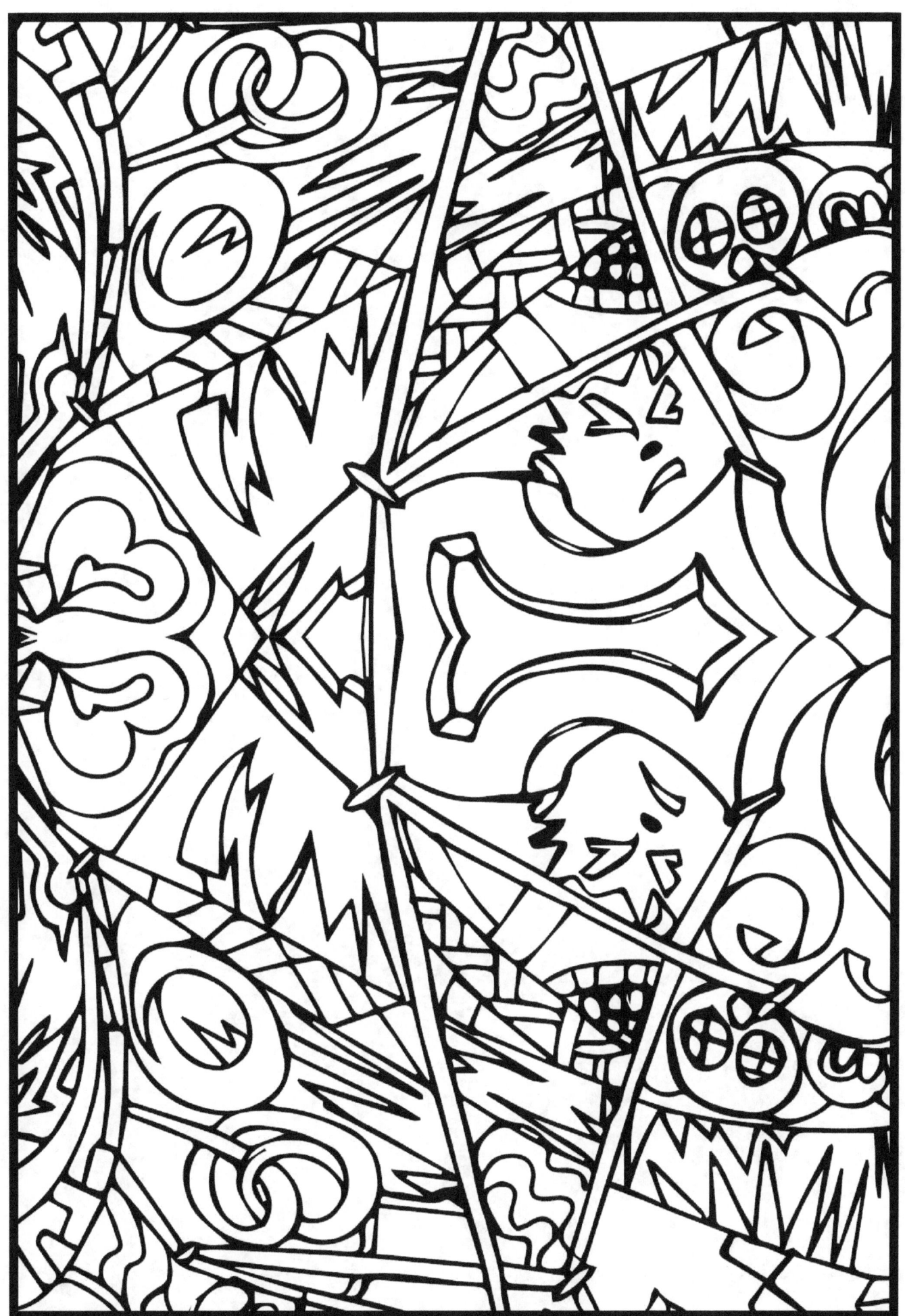

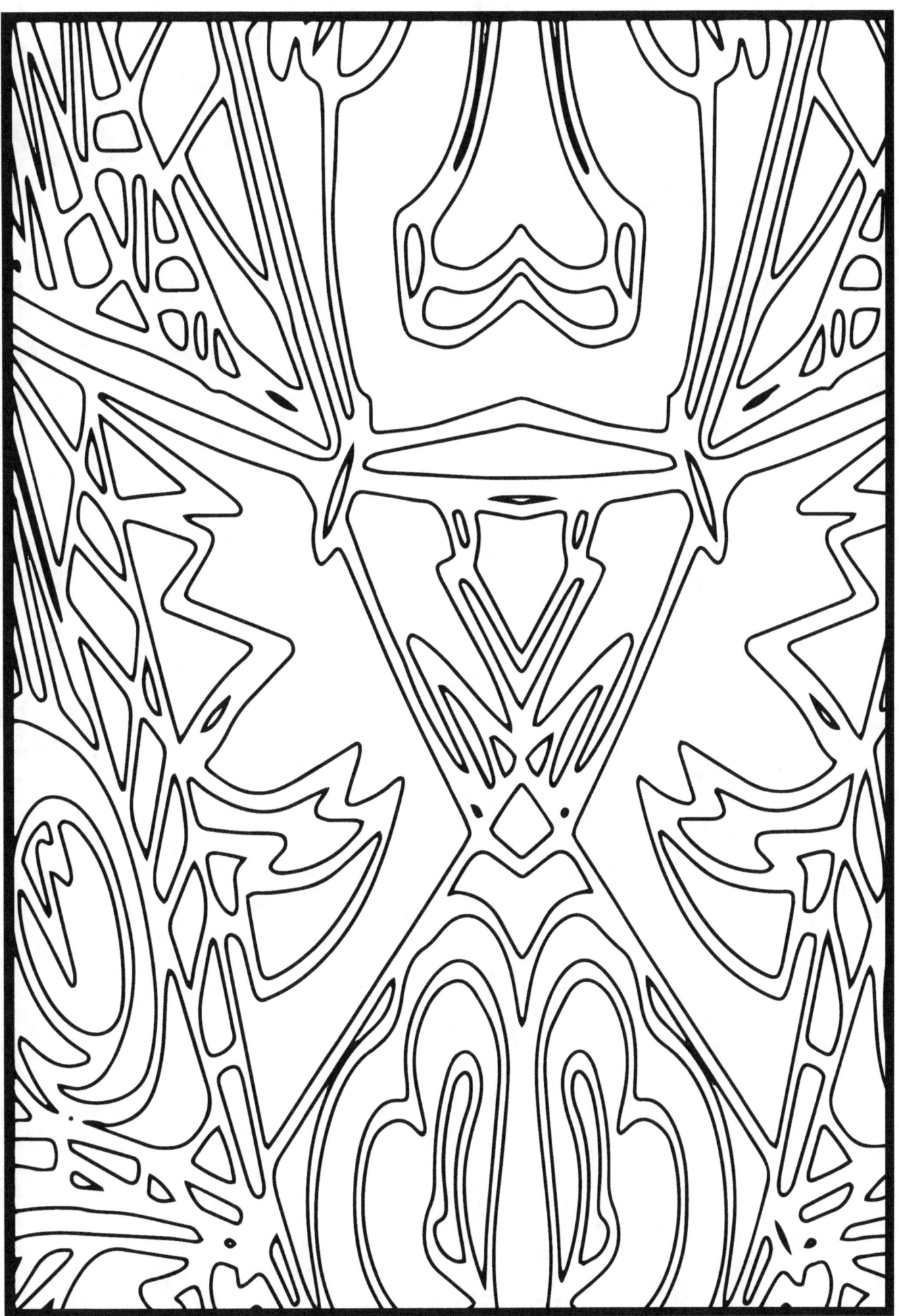

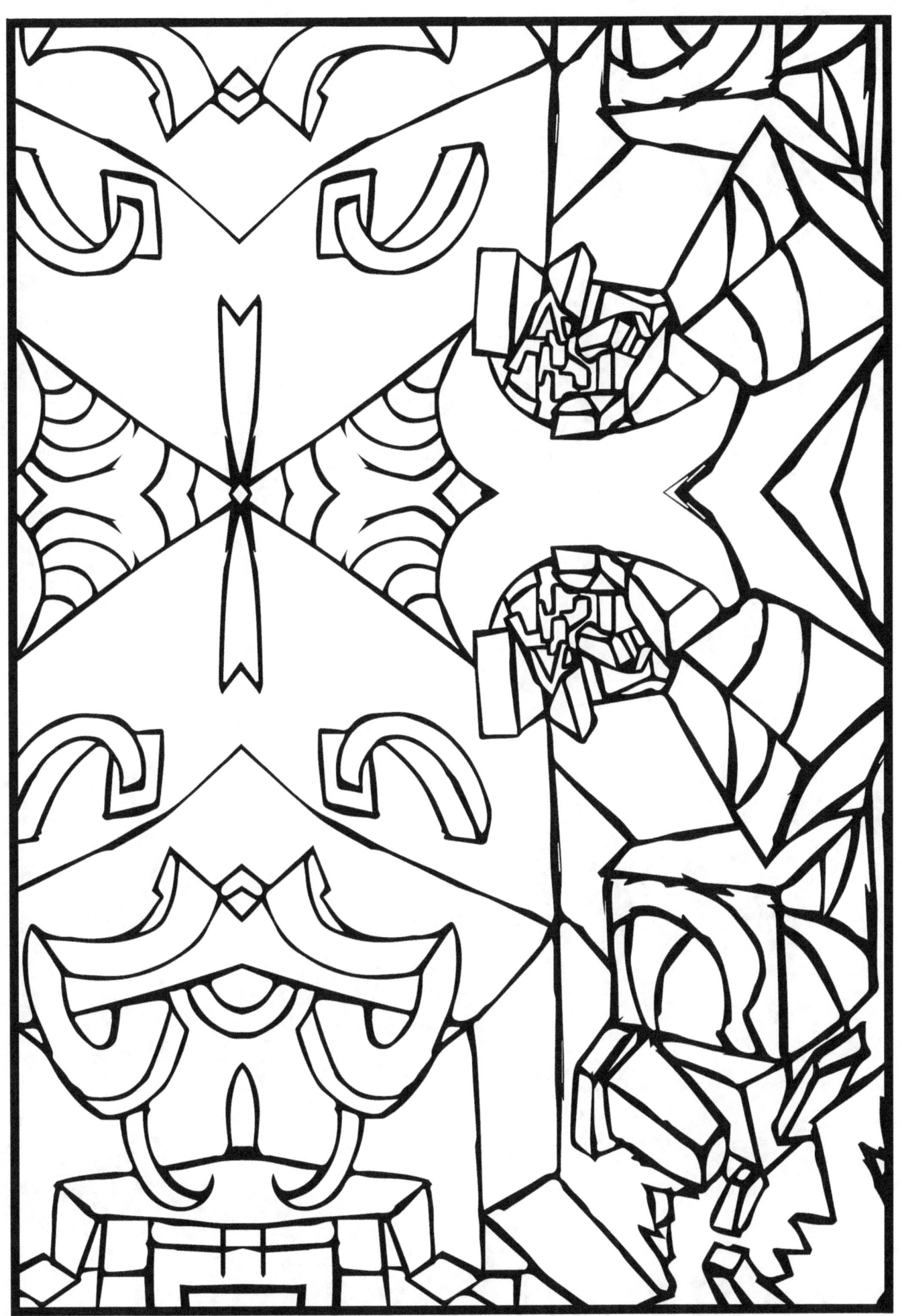

Extra Goodies!

Want more? How fun would it be to see your favorite design bigger and bolder, ready to color so you can create your own masterpiece to share with your friends and family?

From the index below, find the design of your choice, note the number next to it, and go to **www.sashascully.com/journey1discount.html**. On that page, you have the option to purchase a PDF of your design that can be printed up to 24 in. by 36 in.

Need some inspirational ideas for your finished or ready to color designs of your choice? Here are a few to get you started. You can find pictures and videos of examples on my website.

- Create your own family sized poster to color during family night
- Print on canvas to create your own vibrant piece of fine art
- Use your favorite computer art program to create unique digital art
- Create amazing origami

While visiting my website, sign up for my newsletter for occasional surprises such as new products, additional inspirational ideas to use with you favorite designs, special discounts and promotions.

Your journey is limited only by your imagination! Happy coloring!!!

www.sashascully.com

Index of Images Available for PDF Downloads

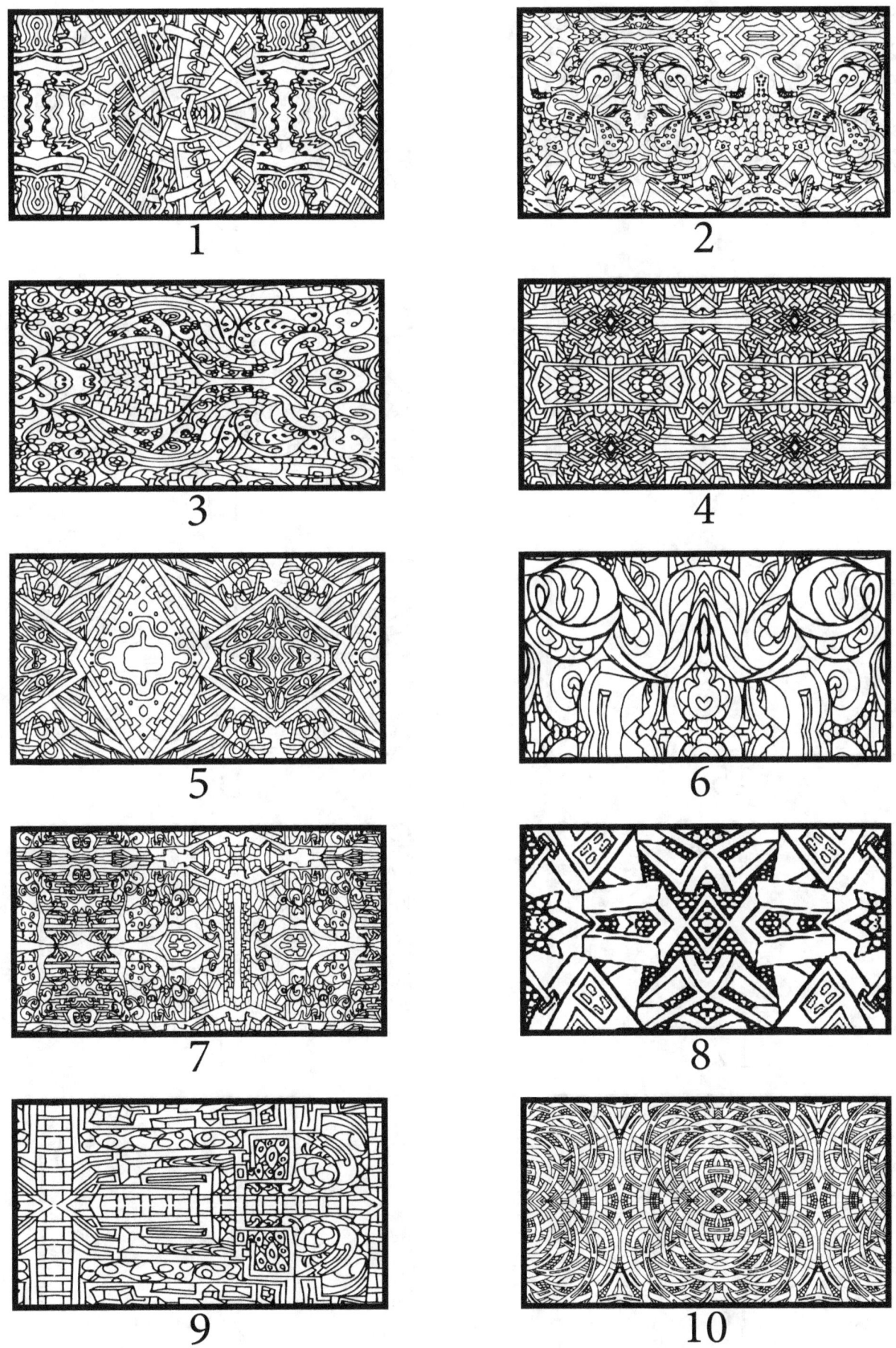

Index of Images Available for PDF Downloads

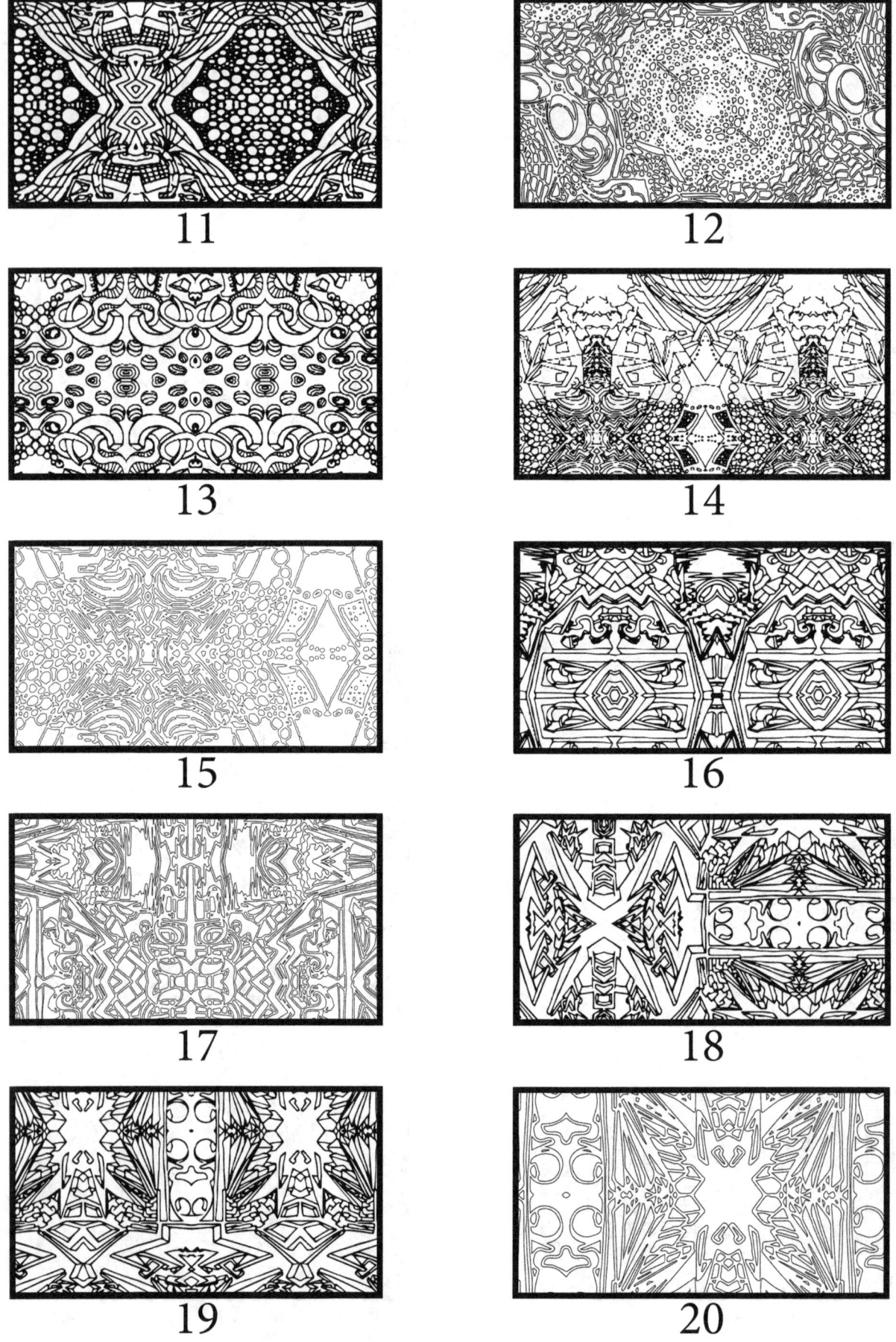

Index of Images Available for PDF Downloads

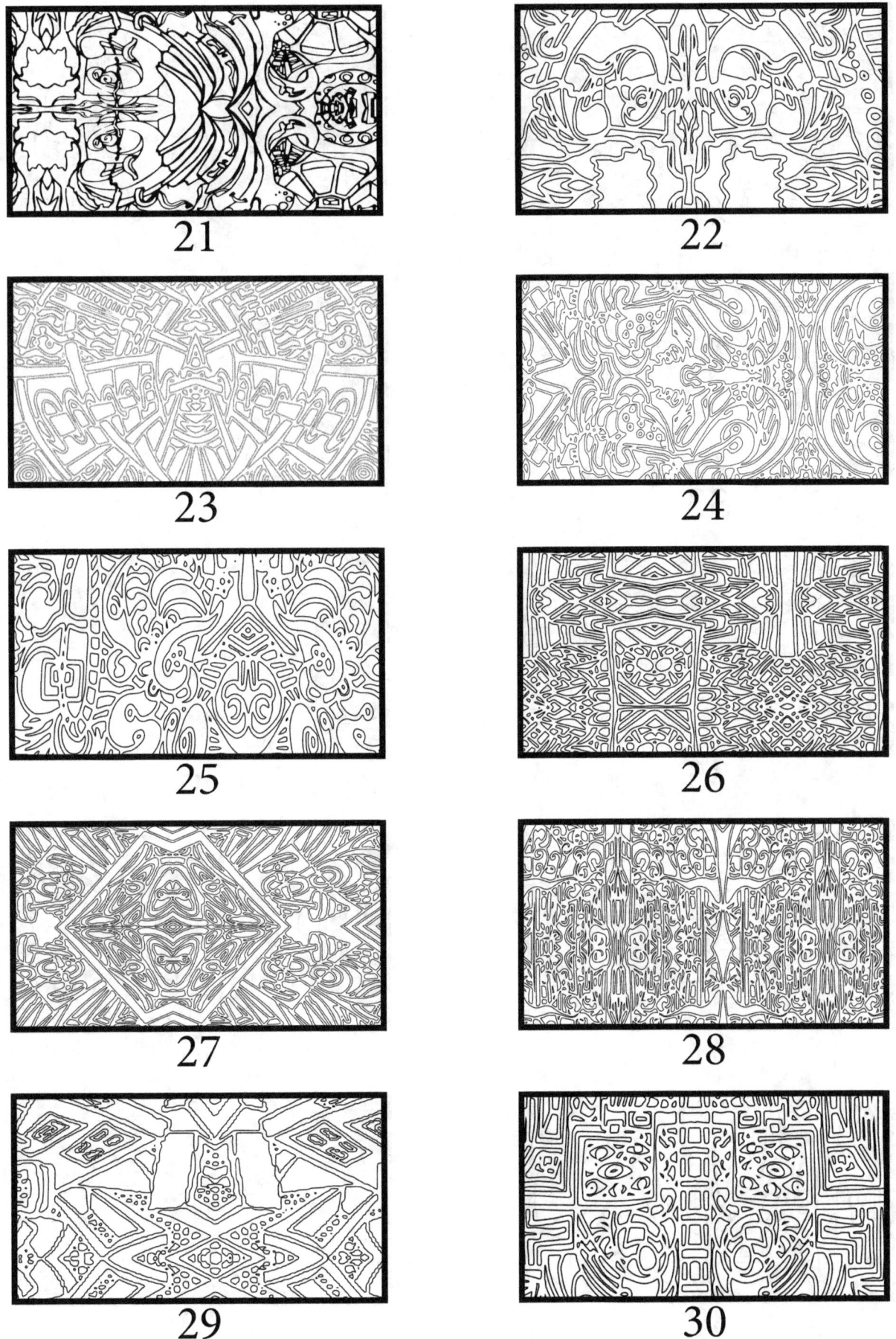

21

22

23

24

25

26

27

28

29

30

Index of Images Available for PDF Downloads

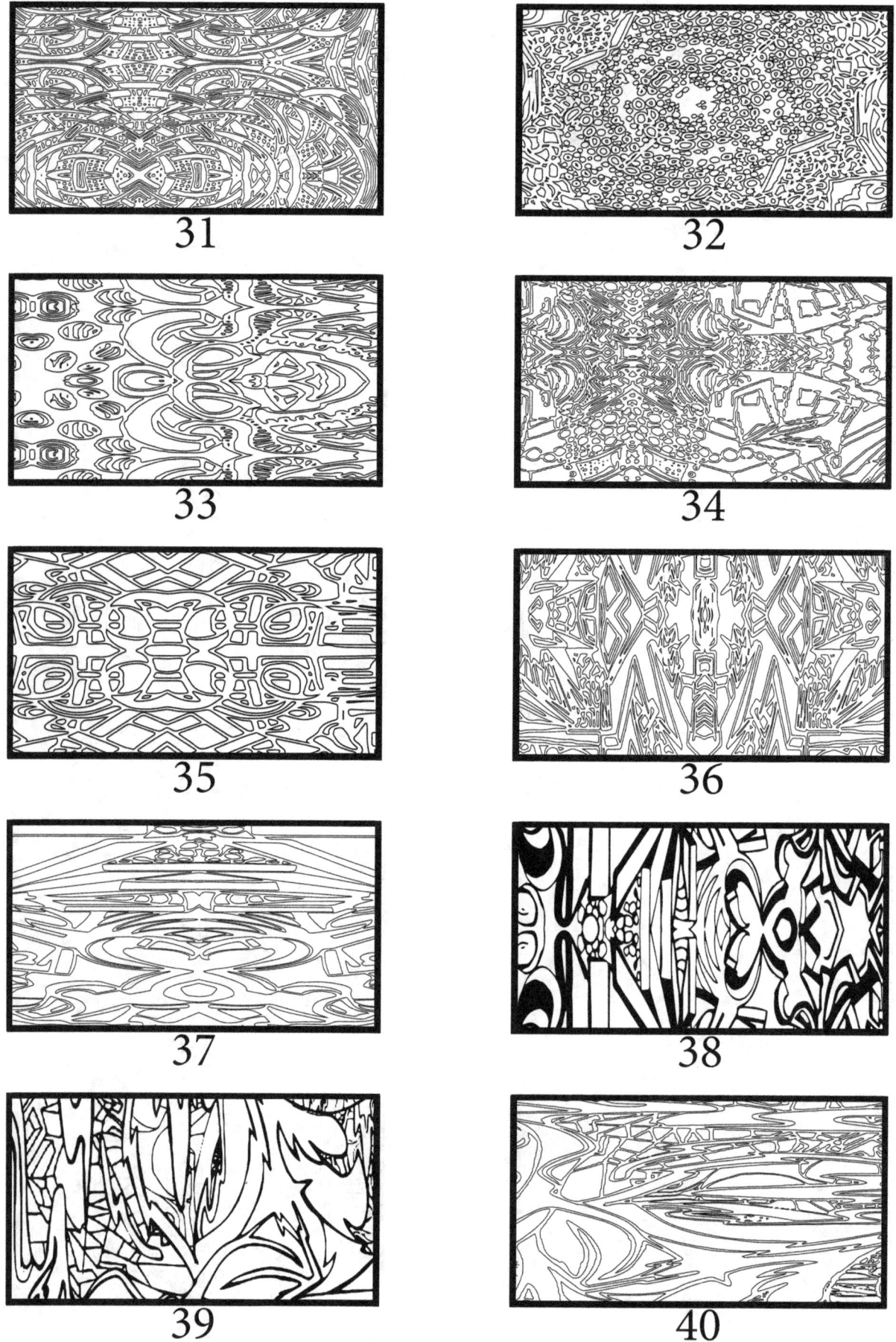

31

32

33

34

35

36

37

38

39

40

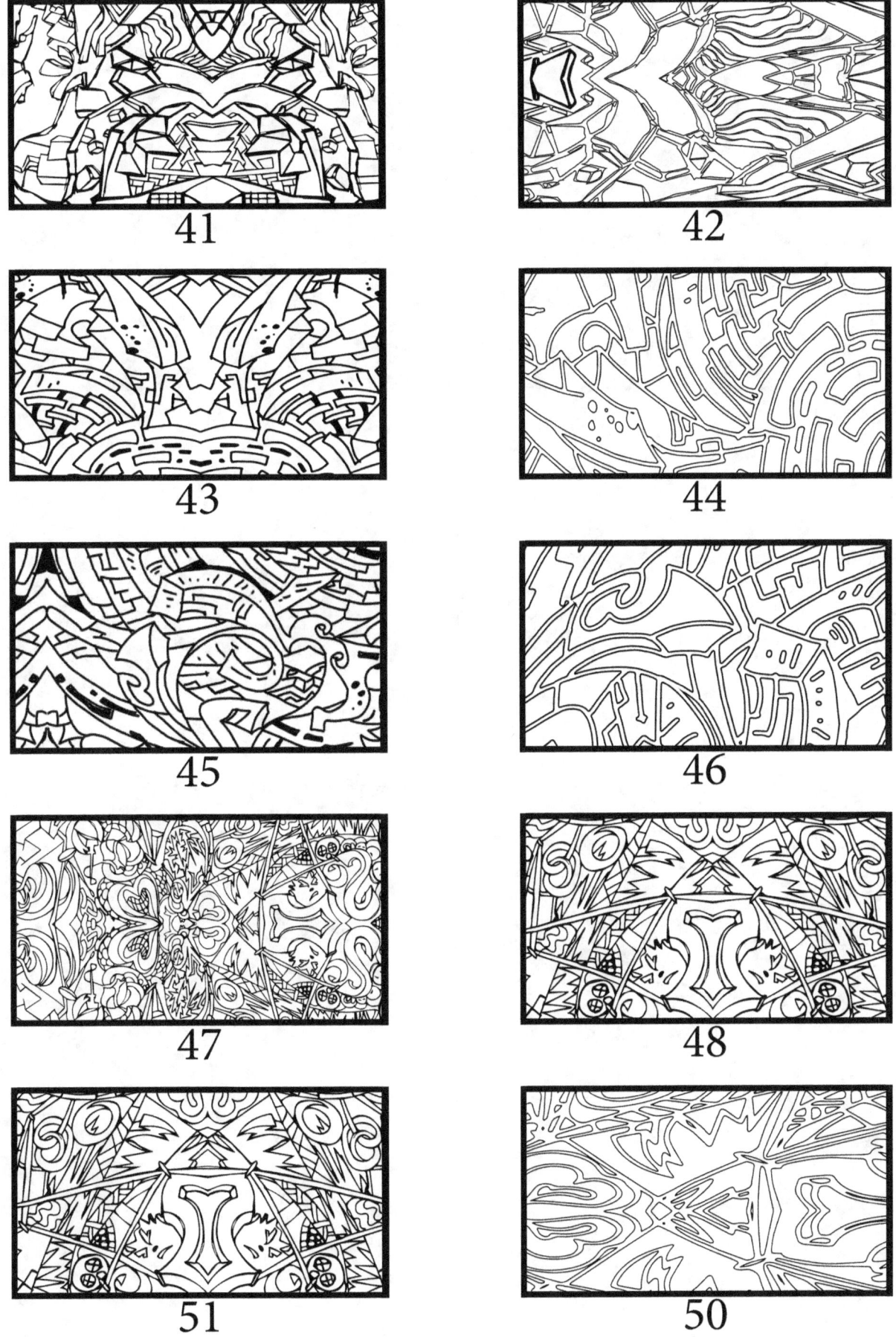

41

42

43

44

45

46

47

48

51

50

SHHHHH..... I am coloring my masterpiece!

www.ingramcontent.com/pod-product-compliance
Lightning Source LLC
Chambersburg PA
CBHW081005170526
45158CB00010B/2916